LogicWorks™ 5

Interactive Circuit Design Software

D1361301

LogicWorks™ 5

Interactive Circuit Design Software

Capilano Computing Systems Ltd.

North Vancouver, BC, Canada

PEARSON

Prentice
Hall

Upper Saddle River, NJ 07458

Library of Congress Cataloging-in-Publication Data

LogicWorks 5 : interactive circuit design software / Capilano Computing Systems Ltd.
  p. cm.
  Includes index.
  ISBN 0-13-145658-X
  1. Logic circuits--Computer-aided design. I. Title: LogicWorks five. II. Capilano
Computing Systems, Ltd.

TK7868.L6L655 2003
621.39'5--dc22   2003061026

Vice President and Editorial Director, ECS: *Marcia J. Horton*
Vice President and Director of Production and Manufacturing, ESM: *David W. Riccardi*
Executive Managing Editor: *Vince O'Brien*
Managing Editor: *David A. George*
Production Editor: *Scott Disanno*
Director of Creative Services: *Paul Belfanti*
Creative Director: *Jayne Conte*
Art Editor: *Greg Dulles*
Manufacturing Manager: *Trudy Pisciotti*
Manufacturing Buyer: *Lisa McDowell*
Marketing Manager: *Holly Stark*

© 2004, 1999 Pearson Education, Inc.
Pearson Prentice Hall
Pearson Education, Inc.
Upper Saddle River, New Jersey 07458

About the Cover: The Capilano Suspension Bridge spans the Capilano Canyon 230 feet above the Capilano River in North Vancouver, British Columbia. Cover image used with permission, © Michael C. Snell, Shade of the Cottonwood, L.L.C.

All rights reserved. No part of this book may be reproduced, in any form or by any means, without permission in writing from the publisher.

Pearson Prentice Hall® is a trademark of Pearson Education, Inc.

LogicWorks is a trademark of Capilano Computing Systems Ltd., North Vancouver, BC, Canada.

Windows is a registered trademark of the Microsoft Corporation, Redmond, WA.

The author and publisher of this book have used their best efforts in preparing this book. These efforts include the development, research, and testing of the theories and programs to determine their effectiveness. The author and publisher make no warranty of any kind, expressed or implied, with regard to these programs or the documentation contained in this book. The author and publisher shall not be liable in any event for incidental or consequential damages in connection with, or arising out of, the furnishing, performance, or use of these programs.

Printed in the United States of America

10 9 8 7 6 5 4 3 2 1

ISBN 0-13-145658-X

Pearson Education Ltd., *London*
Pearson Education Australia Pty. Ltd., *Sydney*
Pearson Education Singapore, Pte. Ltd.
Pearson Education North Asia Ltd., *Hong Kong*
Pearson Education Canada Inc., *Toronto*
Pearson Educación de Mexico, S.A. de C.V.
Pearson Education—Japan, *Tokyo*
Pearson Education Malaysia, Pte. Ltd.
Pearson Education, Inc., *Upper Saddle River, New Jersey*

Contents

3

User Interface 11

4

Tutorial—The Five-Minute Schematic and Simulation 21

5

Tutorial—Schematic Editing 35

6

Tutorial—Structural Simulation 49

7

Tutorial—Using VHDL in LogicWorks 59

8

Tutorial—Creating Device Symbols   79

Part II
The VHDL Language   85

9

Simulation of Digital Systems Using VHDL   87

10

Basic Language Concepts   103

11

Modeling Behavior   135

12

Modeling Structure   177

13
Subprograms, Packages, and Libraries   205

14
Identifiers, Data Types, and Operators   229

Index   241

Preface

Welcome to LogicWorks™ and the world of interactive circuit design. As electronic systems have become more complex, operating speeds higher, and custom chip technology more widespread, software tools for engineers have become an essential part of the design process. It is no longer possible for an individual engineer or a corporation to remain competitive while using pencil and paper for design. Powerful computer-aided design (CAD) programs have been commercially developed to meet the increasing demands facing industry. At Capilano Computing Systems Ltd., our flagship product, Design-Works™, is used in government, industrial, and academic labs worldwide, providing users with speed, ease of use, and affordability. Many instructors want to give their students hands-on experience with CAD tools used in industry, but the high cost and complexity of most commercial CAD programs limit their use at academic institutions. In light of this situation, we developed LogicWorks, the student version of DesignWorks, to be used by students in lab settings and by instructors as an interactive teaching aid. LogicWorks was created with the following goals in mind:

- to give the student an introduction to the concepts and practicalities of using CAD tools;
- to provide a "virtual workbench" that allows the student to quickly test out circuit design ideas and document results;
- to be intuitive and easy to use, so that time is not wasted on the details of installing and operating the software;
- to provide the features and interfaces necessary to work with current design technologies;
- to provide an upward path to professional design tools used in industry.

The major change in LogicWorks 5 from previous versions is the addition of VHDL simulation. VHDL has become the industry standard method for describing digital systems in a high-level language, and an understanding of it is now essential for any working circuit designer. VHDL is a huge language, and LogicWorks does not attempt to provide a full implementation in this version. Our goal is to present the features that are most commonly used and taught, and to keep the package easy to use and low in cost.

Acknowledgments

Many people at Capilano Computing and at Pearson Prentice Hall provided invaluable help in bringing this version of the LogicWorks manual into the world. Particular thanks go out to our editor Tom Robbins at Prentice Hall and to Neil MacKenzie at Capilano, both of whom remained cheerful and fun to work with despite setbacks and schedule pressures. In addition, we would like to acknowledge our many friends and supporters in the academic and industrial worlds who continue to provide valuable feedback and support for the ongoing development of this product.

We deeply appreciate Professor Sudhakar Yalamanchili of Georgia Tech for allowing us to adapt some of the content from his widely used Prentice Hall book, *VHDL Starter's Guide* [0-13-519802-X].

CHRIS DEWHURST
Vancouver, BC, Canada

1

Introduction

Welcome to the world of electronics design using LogicWorks! The purpose of this manual is to get you acquainted as quickly as possible with all the powerful editing and simulation features of the program.

Support on the Internet

Capilano Computing operates an active World Wide Web site for LogicWorks users at **www.logicworks5.com**. Visit the site for program updates, installation assistance, technical support, user-contributed libraries, program add-ons, and up-to-date information on using LogicWorks.

Description of LogicWorks 5

General Features

- Compatible with all current IBM PC–compatible computers running Windows 98 or newer versions.

- Fully interactive operation. Any change to a circuit, input, or device parameter immediately affects displayed circuit activity. The timing diagram is updated and scrolls continuously as the simulation progresses.

- LogicWorks is upward compatible to the full DesignWorks™ professional circuit-design system. All files created in LogicWorks can be read by DesignWorks. The reverse, however, is not true, because of the additional structural features in DesignWorks.

Schematic Drawing Features

■ The symbol editor tool (included with LogicWorks) allows you to create libraries of custom device symbols using familiar drawing tools.

■ Any circuit can be attached to a symbol as a subcircuit to create a simulation model. The subcircuit can be opened at any time to view or modify internal operation.

■ A circuit schematic can be up to a total of 5 feet by 5 feet. Any number of circuit windows can be open simultaneously, allowing easy copying of partial or complete diagrams from one file to another. Each circuit is displayed in a separate window with independent control of scroll and zoom.

■ Commands and drawing modes can be selected using menu items, keyboard equivalents, or a tool palette that is always visible in each window.

■ Any group of objects on the drawing can be repositioned with a simple click–drag mouse action. Signal lines are rerouted interactively to maintain right-angle connections.

■ Multiple signal-line routing methods allow most pin-to-pin connections to be made with only two mouse clicks.

■ Signal names are global across a schematic. Like-named signals are thus logically connected for simulation and netlisting purposes.

■ Free text created in other programs can be pasted onto a circuit schematic. Similarly, complete or partial circuit diagrams can be pasted into word-processing or drafting documents.

■ Objects can be drawn in user-selectable colors on machines equipped with a color display.

■ Circuit and timing diagrams can be printed on any laser, inkjet, or dot-matrix printer that is supported by a Windows device driver.

Simulation Features

■ Full digital simulation capability is provided. Circuit output may be displayed in the form of timing diagrams or on simulated output devices. The program uses 13 signal states, including forcing and resistive drive levels to correctly simulate circuits with design errors such as unconnected inputs or conflicting outputs.

■ Device delay time for individual primitive components may be set to any time value with a resolution of 1 femtosecond.

■ The timing display has adjustable time-per-division and reference-line placement.

■ Common SSI and some MSI devices are implemented as primitives with hard-coded simulation functions. These primitive devices can be used to create higher level device functions and are "scalable," so you can create a 28-input AND gate or a 13-bit counter, for example, as a single primitive device.

■ Test and control devices, such as switches and displays, are active right on the schematic diagram, allowing circuit operation to be directly controlled and observed.

■ A Clock generator device produces signals with variable period and duty cycle. Any number of clock generators can exist in one circuit.

■ Programmable Logic Arrays (PLAs) can be created with up to 256 inputs and 256 outputs with user-specified binary logic. Programmable Read-Only Memories with up to 16 inputs and 128 outputs can also be simulated.

■ A simulation control palette allows the circuit to be single-stepped or run at various speeds.

■ RAM devices of any configuration from 1×1 to 1 Meg $\times$ 64 can be created and simulated (based on available memory). Device options include zero or one OE input, zero to three CE inputs, separate- or combined-data I/O pins, and three-state or normal outputs.

New Features in Version 5

■ A completely new user interface with extensive new on-screen tools and dockable windows is provided.

■ PLA, PROM, and RAM Wizards guide you through the process of creating simulation models for these device types.

- You may add borders and title blocks to circuit diagrams to create finished, professional-looking printed documentation.

- You may paste graphics from any outside drawing program onto the LogicWorks schematic.

Limitations of This Version

- The absolute maximum number of devices in a master circuit or subcircuit is 32,767.

- A typical maximum number of devices without severe performance degradation is 500–2,000, depending on the processor model.

- The maximum length of a pin number is 4 characters.

- The maximum length of a device, pin, or signal name is 16 characters.

- The maximum length of a device-type name is 32 characters.

- The maximum number of pins on a device is 800.

- The entire circuit must fit into available memory.

Where to Start

We suggest you ease yourself into the world of schematic editing and simulation with LogicWorks by taking the following steps:

1. Install the package using the procedures outlined in Chapter 2, "Getting Started," and read all of the "ReadMe" files supplied on the disk with the package.

2. If you are using LogicWorks for the first time, work first through Chapter 4, "Tutorial." It provides step-by-step instructions for basic schematic editing.

3. Refer to Chapter 5, "Schematic Editing," for background on basic editing techniques.

Copyright and Trademarks

The LogicWorks software and manual are copyrighted products. The software license you have purchased entitles you to use the software on a single machine, with copies being made only for backup purposes. Any unauthorized copying of the program or documentation is subject to prosecution.

The names LogicWorks and DesignWorks are trademarks of Capilano Computing Systems Ltd. All other trademarks used are property of their respective owners.

Part I
Using LogicWorks 5

2

Getting Started

This chapter gives you information on installing and starting up LogicWorks.

NOTE: Since the LogicWorks package and the Windows operating system are constantly being upgraded, there may be recent changes and additional updates that you can download for free from our website, **www.logicworks5.com**.

Installation

Procedure

Follow these instructions to install LogicWorks:

◆ Start Microsoft Windows (98, NT, 2000, or XP).

◆ Ensure that LogicWorks is not currently running on the target system.

◆ Insert the LogicWorks CD into your CD drive.

◆ On your Windows desktop, open My Computer and then open the CD drive. Run the LogicWorks5Setup.exe program from the CD by double-clicking on it.

◆ Follow the instructions given on the screen. The installer will then unpack and copy files from the installation disk to your hard disk.

◆   The installer will create a LogicWorks 5 program group under Programs in the Start menu. If a "ReadMe" file's icon also appears,
please read this file, as it will contain any updates to the information printed here.

Getting Started Using LogicWorks

If you are new to LogicWorks, the best place to start is Chapter 4,
"Tutorial—The Five-Minute Schematic and Simulation," starting on
page 21. This chapter will bring you up to speed with the basic program functions. The subsequent chapters contain other tutorials on
specific aspects of the package.

The Initialization File

The LogicWorks initialization file (lw.ini) is a text file that specifies
some initial actions that LogicWorks will take each time it is started
up. The initialization file specifies the following information:

■   which libraries to open when the program is started;

■   which colors to use in displaying objects on the screen;

■   screen fonts, printer parameters, and other options.

The initialization file can be edited (or created anew) by using your
favorite programming editor or word processor. If you use a word
processor, be sure to save the file using a "text only" option. The initialization file must be called lw.ini and must be in the same directory
as the LogicWorks program itself.

◆   For more information on the meaning and format of the
initialization file's contents, see the LogicWorks Reference
Manual provided in electronic form with the software.

3
User Interface

This chapter provides general information on the use of windows, drawing tools, and other user interface features of LogicWorks.

Mouse Button Usage

Three different mouse-button actions are used for various functions in LogicWorks. For clarity, we will use the following terminology when referring to these actions in the remainder of the manual:

Click means press and release the left mouse button without moving the mouse. Example: "To select a device, click on it."

Click and drag means press the left mouse button and hold it down while moving the mouse to the appropriate position for the next action. Example: "To move a device, click and drag it to the desired new position."

Double-click means press and release the left mouse button twice in quick succession without moving the mouse. Example: "To open a device's internal circuit, double-click on the device."

Right-click means press the right mouse button. This action is usually used to display a pop-up "context" menu that allows you to perform operations on the selected item.

Dialog Boxes

Many LogicWorks functions display or request information by displaying a window called a dialog box. For example, the following dialog box is displayed when a Get Info command is executed for a signal:

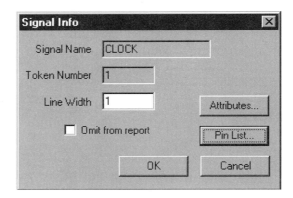

Enter Key

In general, the controls in dialog boxes will behave according to Windows standards, with the following exception: Since some of the boxes require text entry with multiple lines, the (ENTER) key *will not* cause the box to be closed and the default action to be performed in these cases. If the flashing text cursor is currently in a text box that allows multiple-line entry, such as the Attributes dialog, then the (ENTER) key will simply insert a hard return in the text. If the insertion point is located in a text box that does *not* allow multiple lines, then the (ENTER) key will execute the dialog box's default action.

Using the Clipboard in Dialog Boxes

In most dialog boxes requiring text entry, the keyboard equivalents for the Clipboard commands Cut ((CTRL)–X), Copy ((CTRL)–C), and Paste ((CTRL)–V) are active and can be used to transfer text to or from a text box.

Window Usage

Circuit Windows

Each circuit window displays a circuit schematic. The title on a schematic window will be the name of the circuit file displayed in that window (e.g., DESIGN9.CCT). Any number of circuits can be displayed simultaneously. However, at any given time, only one circuit is "current"—the one in the topmost window. Any other window can be made current simply by clicking the left mouse button when the mouse pointer is anywhere in that window.

Timing Windows

When you are simulating a circuit, you can optionally display a Timing diagram window to show signal values versus time. Only one Timing window can be displayed at any given time, and it shows waveforms generated by the current design. Closing the Timing window does not close the circuit design file.

Window Operations

Circuit and Symbol Editor Windows

This table summarizes the common operations on circuit and symbol editor windows:

To...	Do this...
Close the window	Click on the Close icon (the X at the top right corner of the window). If the circuit being closed is the top level of the design (i.e., it isn't an internal circuit of a device symbol), then this action closes the circuit file.

Resize the window	To enlarge or reduce a circuit or symbol editor window; position the mouse pointer along any edge or corner of the window, and click and drag the window to the desired size. As long as the mouse button is held down, a gray outline of the window will track the mouse's movements. When the button is released, the window will be redrawn to the new size and shape.
	To expand the circuit window to fill the whole available area, click on the Maximize button at the upper right corner of the window. Clicking again on this button will cause the window to return to its original size.
Move the window	To move the circuit or symbol editor window, position the mouse pointer on the title bar along the top edge of the window and press and hold the left mouse button. As long as the button is held down, a gray outline of the window will track the mouse's movements. When the button is released, the window will be redrawn at its new position.

Timing, Parts, and Other Docking Windows

The timing window, parts palette, and other display and control windows are referred to as "docking" windows. This means that they can be positioned at one edge of the main application window and will automatically adjust themselves to fit as the main application is moved and resized. This table summarizes the positioning controls for docking windows:

To...	Do this...
Close the window	Click on the Close icon (the X at the top right corner of the window).
Reopen a closed window	Docking windows are normally associated with a specific program function and may not be displayed at all times. The timing window, parts palette, and other commonly used windows have a particular button associated with them on the toolbar. Clicking the appropriate button will show or hide the associated window.

Resize the window	Docking windows can be moved to any edge of the main application window by clicking and dragging in the "gripper bar" of the window. If a docking window is dragged outside the main application, it will "float" as a separate window.
Float the window	Docking windows can be switched to "floating" windows, that is, separate windows that stay above all other windows and can be resized independently. To float a window, right-click in the top bar (near the Close box) of the window and uncheck the "Allow Docking" menu item. You can now move the window to any desired location within or outside of the main application window.

The Window Menu

Selections provided on the Window menu (on the LogicWorks menu bar) can be used to bring to the front any window that is currently open.

Keyboard Usage

The keyboard is absolutely required only when entering names for devices or signals, and for placing free-text notations on a drawing. However, the (CTRL), (SHIFT), and (TAB) keys on the keyboard can be used with many editing operations to invoke special features such as autoalignment, autonaming, and different signal-line drawing methods. In addition, the arrow keys can be used as a convenient way of setting symbol rotation while placing devices or pasting circuit groups. These options are described in detail in the relevant chapters.

Pop-Up Menus

At any time while editing a diagram, you can use the right mouse button to click on a schematic object. A pop-up menu will appear under the cursor, allowing you to select from commands appropriate to that object. For example, the menu for a device contains commands to get device information, edit attributes, open the internal circuit, flip or rotate the symbol, perform Cut and Copy operations, and so on.

Separate pop-up menus are available for devices, signals, pins, attributes, and (if you click on open space on the drawing) the circuit itself.

◆   For details on commands in pop-up menus, see Chapter 12, "Menu Reference."

Toolbars

Toolbars are collections of graphical buttons that remained anchored to the edge of the main program window. They provide direct access to many program functions as an alternative to menu selections. Here is a typical example:

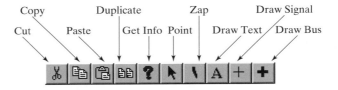

Learning the Tool Functions

Several on-screen hints help you determine the function of a tool that may not be familiar to you. As you move the cursor over a tool, a description of the tool appears in the status bar at the bottom of the screen. In addition, if you pause over a tool, a small window will pop up momentarily with the title of that tool.

Moving the Toolbars

Toolbars can be moved to any desired position on the screen by clicking and dragging anywhere in the toolbar that is not a button. If the toolbar is moved away from the top of the main application window, it will become a floating palette that will stay in front of all other windows.

Hiding a Toolbar

A toolbar can be hidden by either of these methods:

■ Drag the toolbar away from the top of the main application window so that it becomes a floating palette, and then click on its Close (X) icon in the top right corner.

■ Select the associated item in the View menu. The menu item will be checked when the toolbar is showing. Selecting the item will then uncheck it and hide the toolbar.

Use of the Pointer or Cursor

In subsequent descriptions, we will refer to the small on-screen shape that tracks the mouse position as the "pointer" or "cursor." In Logic-Works, there are a number of cursor modes that determine what action will be performed when the left mouse button is clicked. Following is a summary of cursor modes. More detailed descriptions of operations performed in each mode are provided in later reference chapters. Note that the cursor shape sometimes differs from the associated toolbar icon for ease of pointing.

Tool Palette Icon	Initial Cursor Shape	Equivalent Menu Command	Description
▲	▲	Point	Used to select or drag objects and extend signals.
�	�	Zap	Used to remove single objects. Press the left mouse button to remove whatever the tip of the cursor is pointing at. Objects can also be removed in groups by selecting them and using the Clear command or Delete key.
T	✐	Text	Used to select a signal or device to name, or to place free text on the diagram. Point at the item you want to name; and press and hold the left mouse button. Move the cursor to where you want the name to appear, and then release the button.

✚	✖	Draw Bus	Used to create a new bus line or extend an existing bus. Clicking once fixes a corner; double-clicking terminates the line.
✛	✕	Draw Sig	Used to create a new signal line or extend an existing signal. Clicking once fixes a corner; double-clicking terminates the line. Note that most signal-drawing operations can also be done in Point mode.
⚲	⚲	Magnify	Used to zoom in and out. Clicking on a point or dragging down and right zooms in. Dragging up and left zooms out.
⊘	⊘	Signal Probe	Used to view and change signal values on the schematic. Click on the signal to view with the end of the probe, and the cursor will follow changes in the signal's value. Type 0 or 1 on the keyboard to enter a value. See Chapter 7, "Simulation" for more information.

Parts Palette

Parts library contents are displayed in a floating palette window that looks like the following:

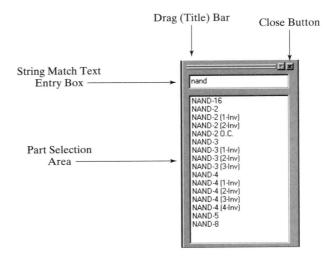

The Parts Palette displays the contents of all parts available in all open library files and allows any item to be selected for placement in the schematic.

Moving the Parts Palette

The Parts Palette can be moved to any desired location on the screen by clicking and dragging its title bar.

Hiding the Parts Palette

The Parts Palette can be removed from the screen by clicking on its Close button. To redisplay the palette, select the Parts Palette command from the View menu.

Choosing a Library

The Parts Palette displays the contents of all open library files, merged into a single list. Library files are opened by selecting the Open command in the Parts Palette pop-up menu, discussed in an upcoming section.

Selecting a Part

Use the following steps to select a part for placement in a schematic:

- If necessary, use the scroll bar to scroll through the list until the desired part name is in view.
- Double-click on the part name in the list.
- Move the cursor to the current schematic window to place the part in it.

Using the String-Matching Box

The string-matching text box allows you to type characters that will reduce the size of the list and make it easier to locate the desired part. Simply click in the text box and type the desired characters. After a brief pause, the displayed part list will be reduced to only those parts that contain the typed string of characters.

To return to the full selection, click at the end of the string of characters in the box and backspace over them until the box is cleared.

Parts Palette Pop-Up Menu

The Parts Palette pop-up menu can be activated by clicking the right mouse button when the cursor is in this window. This menu allows you to open, close, and manage your libraries.

◆ See Chapter 12, "Menu Reference," for specific information on these items.

4

Tutorial—The Five-Minute Schematic and Simulation

This tutorial is divided into a number of sections, allowing you to review the basic functions first and then learn about more advanced features. The first section is entitled "The Five-Minute Schematic and Simulation" and will give you a taste of how quickly you can put together a circuit with full simulation. The later sections are divided by subject, so that you can study in greater detail the features that are important for your application.

These tutorials are intended only to introduce you to LogicWorks features. For complete details on any subject, see the reference sections of this manual.

Tutorial Manual Format

In the following tutorial sections, text with a diamond,

◆   like this,

provides step-by-step instructions for achieving a specific goal. Other text provides background and explanation of the actions being taken.

The Five-Minute Schematic and Simulation

In this section, we're going to show how quickly you can use Logic-Works to create and test a circuit.

Starting LogicWorks

◆ Start the LogicWorks program by double-clicking on its icon.

Once the program has started, you will be looking at a screen like this:

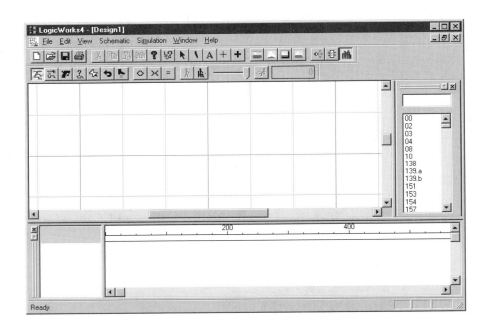

The Circuit window is your viewport onto the circuit diagram, which you will manipulate using the various drawing tools. The smaller panel at the bottom of the screen will be used by the program to display a timing diagram of the signals in your circuit, as well as other outputs generated by your circuit. Either of these windows can be moved or resized by the usual methods to suit your needs.

Placing a Device

The Parts Palette shows a merged list of all parts in all open libraries. Libraries can be opened and closed manually by using the Parts Palette pop-up menu's Open and Close commands, or any collection of libraries can be opened automatically at start-up by placing them in the Libs directory. The Parts Palette appears as follows:

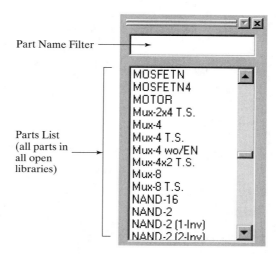

Part Name Filter

Parts List
(all parts in all open libraries)

The list of open libraries can be changed manually by doing either of the following:

■ Click on the File menu and select the Libraries submenu; then choose the New Lib or Open Lib commands as needed.

■ Right-click on the Parts Palette, and use the same set of library commands that appears in that menu.

Any collection of libraries can be opened automatically at start-up by modifying the INI file. This procedure is described in more detail in the LogicWorks reference manual provided in electronic form with the software.

◆ Locate the Filter text box on the Parts Palette. Type the text 164 into this box. This step will reduce the parts list to only items containing that text.

◆ Locate the part 74_164 in the parts list, and double-click on it.

◆ Move the cursor back into the circuit window. The cursor on the screen will now be replaced by a moving image of the selected symbol, in this case an 8-bit shift register.

The numbered devices in this library are generic 7400-series types. The labeling and simulation characteristics can be adjusted to match the various 7400 families on the market.

◆ Position this image somewhere near the center of the circuit window, and click the left mouse button. A permanent image of the device will now stay behind in that location, and the cursor image will continue to follow the movements of the mouse:

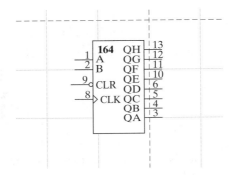

More devices of the same type could be created at this point, but in this example we wish to select another symbol:

◆ Press the spacebar to return to Point mode. Notice that you can click and drag the device that you placed to any desired new position.

◆ Move again to the Parts Palette, and this time double-click on the XNOR-2 type. (You might need to change the text in the "Filter" box, if you used it in a previous step.) Once you move outside of the Parts Palette, the cursor will immediately change to match the new symbol.

The XNOR-2 and the devices in the Simulation Gates, Simulation Logic, and Simulation I/O libraries are called primitive types because they have built-in simulation models in LogicWorks. Other devices, such as those in the 7400 library, are called subcircuit types, because their simulation models are made up of primitives. If LogicWorks is being used only for schematic entry, it is also possible to make symbols with no simulation function:

◆ Place one of these Exclusive-NOR gates adjacent to the 164 device so that the pins just touch, and click once to anchor the device.

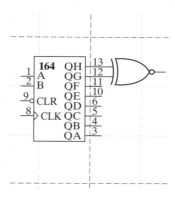

◆ Press the spacebar to return to Point mode.

Whenever you place devices or signal lines so that they touch, you will notice that the signal lines flash briefly. This indicates that a logical connection has been made. You do not need to explicitly request a connection.

Moving a Device

◆ Point at the Exclusive NOR gate, and click and drag to the right. While you hold the left mouse button, you can drag the device to any desired new position. Note that any signal lines attached to the device are adjusted continuously to maintain connection.

◆ Position the gate to the right of the 164 device so that it appears as follows:

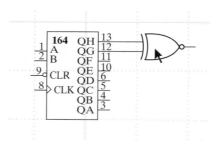

Drawing Signal Connections

◆ Attach a connection to the output of the gate by positioning the pointer near the endpoint of the pin and dragging away to the upper left:

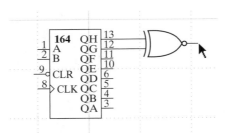

◆ Notice that two lines at right angles will follow your mouse movements to connect the starting and ending points.

While moving the mouse, try pressing the (CTRL) or (ALT) key, and note the different line-routing methods available. Click the left mouse button once to anchor the signal line. For details on these line-routing modifier keys, see the section on signal-line editing in the LogicWorks reference manual provided in electronic form with the software.

◆ Leave a right-angle line attached to the gate as follows:

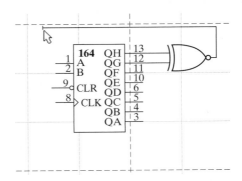

◆ Extend this line to connect to the B input of the 164 by clicking at the line endpoint where you left off, dragging the line to the B input, and releasing the mouse button:

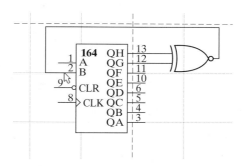

◆ Add a connection to pin A by clicking at the end of the pin, dragging the line down until it touches the signal line, and then releasing the mouse button:

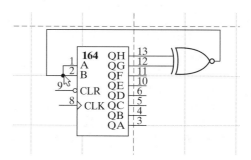

Notice that an intersection dot appears automatically whenever three or more lines intersect.

◆ Try repositioning a line segment by clicking and dragging anywhere along the length of the segment except at a corner or intersection.

Binary Switch Input Device

◆ Return to the Parts Palette and select a Binary Switch device.

◆ Place it as shown on the following diagram:

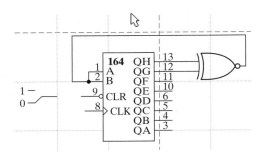

◆ Press the spacebar to return to Point mode.

◆ Try clicking on the switch. Notice that it changes between the 0 and 1 states.

In order to move a switch, you must first select it by holding the SHIFT key while clicking on it. This is necessary because the switch has a special response to a normal mouse click.

The devices in the Simulation I/O library can be used to actively control and observe the simulation right on the schematic. Each of these devices responds immediately to changes in the simulation in progress. The Hex Keyboard device is similar to the switch except that it operates on four lines at once.

Clock Generator Device

◆ Select a Clock device and place it on the diagram just below the switch.

◆ Press the spacebar to return to Point mode.

◆ Route wires from the switch and clock to the 164, as shown in the following diagram (remember to try using the CTRL and ALT keys to route the wires):

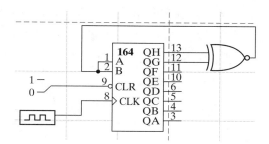

While you have been working on the diagram, the LogicWorks simulator has been running continuously, simulating the effects of the new connections that are being made. So far, though, we have not asked it to display any results. This is done either by placing probes on the diagram or by displaying signals in the Timing window.

Naming a Signal

◆ Click on the text tool in the Tool Palette. The cursor will then change to a pencil shape, which will be used to select the item we want to name.

Text Tool

The text cursor is used to name devices and signals, to apply pin numbers to device pins, and to add free-text notations to the diagram.

◆ Position the tip of the pencil anywhere along the length of the line running from the clock device, and click. A blinking insertion marker will appear:

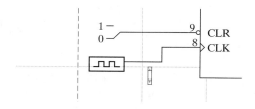

◆ Type the name CLK on the keyboard and then press the (ENTER) key or click the left mouse button once outside the text box.

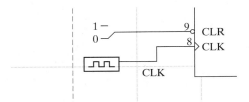

◆ Return to Point mode by clicking the arrow icon in the Tool Palette. Note that the name can be dragged to any desired position.

◆ Click once on the Binary Switch to change it to the logical 1 state.

The Timing Window

You will immediately see the Timing window come to life, with the displayed values on the CLK line:

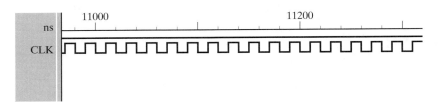

By default, any named signal is shown automatically in the Timing window, although you can change this setting by using the Add Automatically command in the Simulation menu.

◆ Again using the text cursor, name the two data lines from the shift register and the output line from the gate as follows:

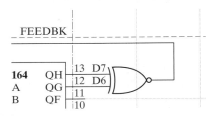

The simulated output from these lines will immediately appear in the Timing window.

Simulation Controls

Click on the <> and >< buttons, and observe that they affect the time scale of the Timing window.

The display resolution can be adjusted over a wide range of time values to suit the displayed data.

◆ Select the Timing Window item in the View menu. You will notice that the Timing window disappears and the current time indicator in the Simulator palette advances much more quickly.

◆ Select the Timing Window command again or use the corresponding ![button] button to reenable the display.

◆ Click on the Reset (![button]) button, and notice that the simulation restarts at time 0.

◆ Adjust the speed slider control in the Simulator toolbar, and notice that simulation slows.

◆ Click on repeatedly on the Step (![button]) button, and observe that the simulation proceeds one step at a time.

◆ Click on the Run button in the Simulator toolbar.

NOTE: The Step button advances the simulation to the next time at which there is some circuit activity, not necessarily just one time unit. The size of the step will depend upon the circuit.

Probe Device

◆ Select the Binary Probe type from the Parts Palette.

◆ Place a probe so that its pin contacts a signal line to view the simulation value on that line:

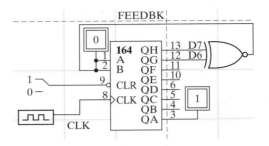

As the simulation progresses, the values on all probes are updated immediately. A similar device, the Hex Display, is also available to show groups of lines in hexadecimal. These simulation devices can be flagged to indicate that they are not a real part of the finished product and should not be included in any netlists or bills of materials.

Setting Device Parameters

◆ Click in the window, but away from any circuit objects. This deselects everything.

◆ Click on the XNOR gate to select it:

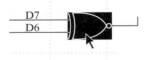

◆ Select the Simulation Params command in the Simulation menu.

◆ Use the controls in this box to increase the propagation delay in the device to 5 ns:

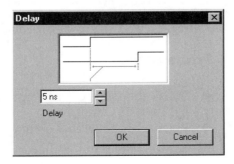

The Simulation Params command is used to view and set delays associated with devices and pins. Pin delays normally default to zero, but can be used to fine-tune the delays for different paths through a device.

◆ Click on the OK button.

Device Delay on the Timing Window

Notice that the altered device delay immediately affects the simulation. You will see an increased delay between the clock reference lines and the changes in the FEEDBK signal:

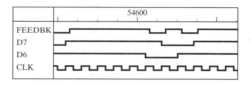

Interacting with the Simulation

◆ Try clicking on the switch hooked to the CLR input:

Notice that it changes state and immediately affects the displayed simulation results.

Saving the Design

Click the Save button ( ) to save your circuit so you can continue with it later.

This ends the Five-Minute Schematic and Simulation tutorial section.

5
Tutorial—Schematic Editing

The object of this tutorial is to take a closer look at LogicWorks's schematic editing features. We will do this by making a number of modifications to the circuit file created in the Five-Minute Schematic and Simulation demonstration.

The topics covered in this section are as follows:

- deleting and moving objects;
- selecting device types by name;
- device symbol rotation;
- using power and ground connectors;
- connecting signals by name;
- using Copy and Paste on circuit objects;
- naming devices;
- adding pin numbers to devices;
- placing text notations on the diagram.

Opening a Circuit File

◆ Open the file you created in the initial demonstration by clicking on the Open button (🖼) or selecting the Open command in the File menu, or open the file that was supplied with LogicWorks in the Examples folder.

◆ If the simulator is running, click the Stop (🛑) button to turn it off, as we will only be looking at schematic editing tools for now.

Deleting and Trimming Objects

◆   Select the Zap () tool in the toolbar. The cursor will change to match this icon.

This tool is used to remove a single object from the diagram. When clicked on a device, the device is removed. When clicked on a signal line, the line segment is removed to the nearest device pin or intersection.

Zap Tool

◆   Zap the segment shown.

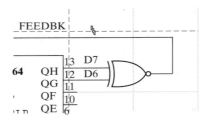

The signal has now been broken into two pieces. The signal name FEEDBK may become associated with the closest piece or might be deleted automatically if it is too far from any of the remaining segments. You can click on the name to see which piece gets highlighted.

Rotating a Device

◆   In the Parts Palette, double-click on the device Buffer-1 O.C. (in the Simulation Logic library). Move the mouse pointer over to the Schematic window.

◆   Before placing the device, try pressing the arrow keys on the keyboard. Notice that the arrow keys change the orientation of the device symbol that is moving on the screen:

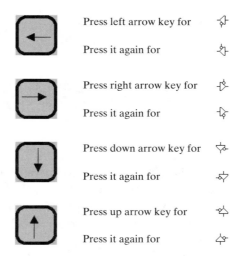

There are actually eight different orientations available: the four major compass points, plus these directions with an additional flip around the major axis. The orientation also applies when groups of objects are pasted or duplicated.

Placing a Device

◆ Place one of the open-collector buffers on the diagram as shown:

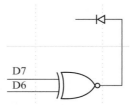

The open-collector buffer is a device that converts a low input into a low-impedance output, and a high input to a high-impedance output. How this device works in conjunction with a pullup resistor will be demonstrated in the following sections.

Resistor Device

◆ In the Parts Palette, select a Resistor device, orient it, and place it as shown.

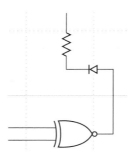

The Resistor device has special properties in the digital simulation. It conducts signal values in both directions, but its output has a lower drive level than its input. Thus, it can be used as a pullup or pulldown resistor in circuit logic, or as a series resistor to simulate low-drive-level devices.

Power and Ground Connectors

◆   Select a +5V device from the Parts Palette and place it as shown:

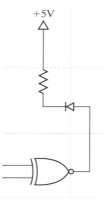

The +5V symbol is called a Signal Connector and performs several functions: It puts out a constant high level for use in the simulation, it assigns the name Plus5V to the attached signal line, and it creates a logical connection to all other signal lines that have the same symbol attached. You can create your own Signal Connectors for commonly used signals by using the symbol editor tool.

◆   Press the spacebar to reactivate the arrow pointer, and then wire these devices together as shown.

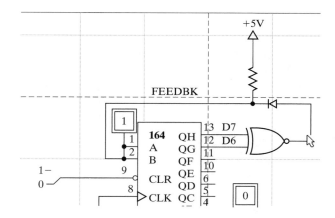

Dragging Groups of Devices

◆ Select the three symbols highlighted in the following diagram by
SHIFT–clicking on them:

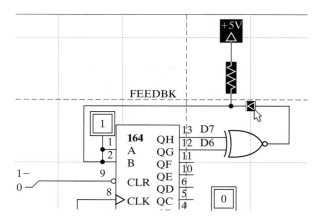

◆ Drag the selected items up away from the 164 device to any convenient location.

Connecting Signals by Name

◆ Select a NOT (Inverter) from the Parts Palette, and place it below
the 164 device as shown.

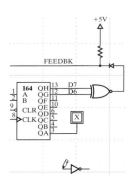

◆ Select the Text (**A**) tool, and name the input on the NOT device as D7 as described in the introductory demo. Be careful to click the pencil cursor at the *end* of the pin. Clicking in the middle of the pin will create a pin number.

When you place the label D7, you will notice that this line will flash, indicating that a logical connection has been made. For simulation and netlisting purposes, these two signals are now connected together. Any like-named signals are considered to be connected.

◆ Double-click on either of the D7 signal lines (that is, along the line segments, not on the name itself) to check connectivity. (Both lines will change color.)

◆ Label the output of the inverter as NOTD7, and observe the inverted signal in the Timing window.

Using Copy and Paste

Now we will use the clipboard commands to copy a section of the circuit to a new circuit file.

◆ Select the group of circuitry to be copied by clicking and dragging across the group of objects. Any object that intersects or is contained within the rectangle will be selected, such as in this diagram:

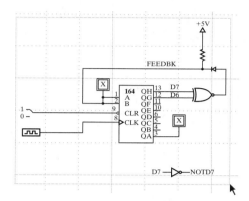

◆ Select the Copy command from the Edit menu.

◆ Select the New command in the File menu, and choose the Circuit option.

◆ Select the Paste command in the Edit menu.

An outline of the entire circuit will now follow your mouse movements. You can place this group of objects anywhere on the new diagram. You can also use the arrow keys to reorient the circuit group before placing it.

The Cut, Copy, Paste, and Duplicate commands can be used on any single object or any group of selected objects.

◆ Select Close Circuit on the File Menu to close the extra copy of the circuit without saving. The original circuit window should still be open.

Naming Devices

Devices are named in a manner similar to signals:

◆ Select the Text (**A**) tool in the toolbar.

◆ With the pencil inside the device, click the left mouse button.

◆ Type the desired name.

◆ Press the (ENTER) key or click the left mouse button once.

◆ Repeat the above steps to name the devices as shown.

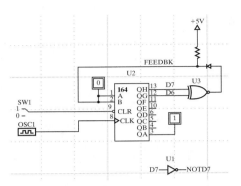

Device or signal names can be moved after they have been placed, by dragging them with the pointer. They can also be edited by clicking in an existing name with the pencil cursor.

Device names are used not only as labels on the schematic, but also in component lists and bills of materials.

Setting Device Attributes

◆ Right-click the Clock device.

◆ In the pop-up menu, select the Attributes command.

LogicWorks has a fixed number of different attribute "fields" that you can use to store auxiliary device information like component values.

◆ Click on the Value item in the field list.

◆ Type the value 14.288 MHz in the text box, as shown.

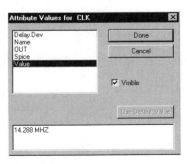

◆ Verify that the Visible option is turned on.

◆ Click the Done button.

Notice that the value that you typed in has now appeared adjacent to the selected device. This text can be moved to any desired location relative to the device.

IMPORTANT: This value is a text annotation only and has no effect on the simulation of the device. Use the Simulation Params command to set simulation values.

Pin Numbering

◆ Select the Text cursor again, and click it on a signal line very close to a device symbol, as shown.

A blinking insertion marker will appear immediately next to the device.

◆ Type up to four digits or letters for the pin number, and then press the (ENTER) key or click the left mouse button once.

Pin numbers can be positioned only directly on device pins and cannot be moved. Pin numbers are used to distinguish device pins when a netlist is created. Most nonprimitive library devices have pin numbers already defined for the most common package type. The default pin numbers can be specified in the symbol library, or they can be edited right on the diagram.

Placing Text on the Diagram

The Text cursor can also be used to place free-text notations anywhere on the diagram.

◆ Click on the diagram with the Text tool, but not near any device or signal line, and a blinking insertion marker will appear at that point.

◆ Type any desired text, using hard returns to create multiple lines.

◆ Click the left mouse button once to terminate typing of the text item. The result should look as follows:

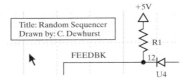

◆ Right-click on the text block that was just created, and select the Properties command. This command allows you to set the text font, color, framing, and other visual aspects of the text notation.

Creating a Bus

A "bus" is a single line on the schematic that represents a group of related signals.

◆ Using the editing techniques we have covered so far, move the XNOR, NOT, and Probe devices to the right as shown in the following diagram (exact position is not important):

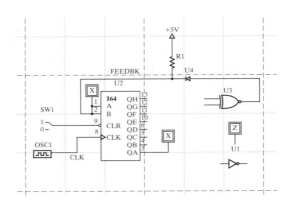

◆ Remove all lines and signal names connecting to the outputs of the 164. Also remove the label from the NOTD7 device (using the Zap tool). This will leave room to create the bus connections.

◆ Select the New Breakout command in the Schematic menu.

A "breakout" is a special symbol that indicates connections between regular signal lines and bus lines. The only way to connect a signal line into a bus is to use a breakout.

◆ Type the text D0..7 (the second character is a zero, not the letter O) into the pin list box as shown in the following screen shot:

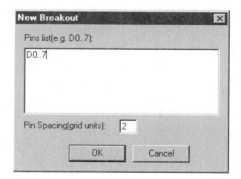

◆ If necessary, change the pin spacing to match the illustration.

◆ Click the OK button.

The text D0..7 tells LogicWorks to create a breakout with eight signals: D0, D1, D2, etc., up to D7. The signals don't have to be sequentially numbered. You can also type any collection of names separated by spaces or commas, such as CLK ENABLE CTRL.

◆ Place the new breakout symbol as shown so that its pins just make contact with the eight outputs of the 164. You will have to use the left arrow key on the keyboard to orient it in the direction shown.

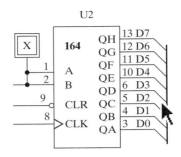

◆ Press the spacebar to reactivate the arrow cursor.

◆ Drag the breakout symbol a little to the right to make more room for the signal names and pin numbers. This is done by clicking in the diagonal-line area of the breakout symbol.

A breakout can be treated just like a device symbol for editing purposes. The diagonal-line area is the breakout symbol. The wide "backbone" of the breakout symbol is actually a bus line. You can now extend the bus in either direction from the breakout just by clicking and dragging at either end of the bus line.

◆ Use the New Breakout command three more times to create small breakouts as shown. For the top one, type "D6 D7" or "D6..D7". For the middle one, type just "D0" and for the bottom one, type "D7".

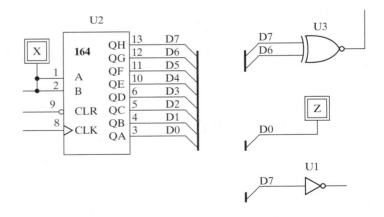

IMPORTANT: Signals are *not* connected by name between different busses. At this point, we have three *different* signals called D7 that are not connected together. They will become connected together in the next step when we join the busses.

◆ Using the arrow cursor, join the bus connections of all the break-outs together as shown in the following diagram. Connect one breakout to the next; do not try to connect all three at once.

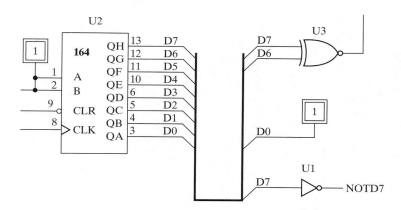

◆ Verify that the circuit still simulates correctly now that the connections are made through busses instead of directly. You may need to use the Clear Unknowns ( ) button in the toolbar to remove any X values that appeared when we broke some of the connections.

◆ Save the file you have created to this point for use later on.

This ends the tutorial section on general schematic editing.

6

Tutorial—Structural Simulation

This section of the tutorial will provide you with a closer look at the integrated digital simulator in LogicWorks, including the following topics:

- types of devices simulated;
- controlling the simulation;
- representation of time and signal values;
- using the trigger;
- using the signal probe.

Logic States

◆ Create a new circuit, using the New command in the File menu.

◆ Create the following partial circuit, using the Buffer-1 O.C. and Binary Probe devices:

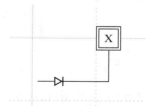

LogicWorks uses a total of 13 different logic values for signals in order to handle different drive levels and unknown situations. The probe will display an X for any of the six possible "Don't Know" states. In this case, the X results from the fact that the device input is unconnected.

◆ Add a Binary Switch device to the input of the buffer as shown.

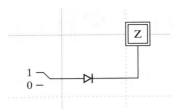

◆ Click on the switch a couple of times, and note that the buffer output alternates between the 0 and Z states.

The Z value indicates a high-impedance or undriven line. Multiple open-collector or three-state devices can drive a line to simulate bus or wired-AND logic.

Circuits with Feedback

◆ Click on the Buffer device, and use the Duplicate command in the Edit Menu to create another one as shown.

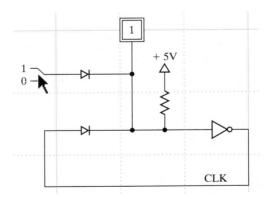

◆ Add a pull-up resistor (using the Resistor and +5V symbols) and an inverter (NOT in the Simulation Gates library), and wire them as shown above.

◆ Click on the switch, and notice the oscillation that occurs due to the feedback in this circuit.

◆ Name the output signal CLK so that it shows in the Timing window.

Using the Signal Probe Tool

◆   Click on the Signal Probe tool in the toolbar:

◆   Click the tip of the Signal Probe tool along any signal line, as
    demonstrated in the following diagram:

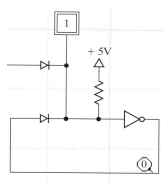

It will show the current value of the signal as the simulation progresses.

You can also use this tool to enter new signal values by typing 0 or 1
on the keyboard while the left mouse button is pressed. Stuck-at,
unknown, and high-impedance levels can also be inserted.

Time Values

LogicWorks uses integers to represent simulated time values. The
smallest unit of time is the femtosecond, written as fs; it denotes 10^{-15}
seconds. Most devices included with LogicWorks default to a delay of
1 ns (nanosecond, or 10^{-9} second).

LogicWorks uses an *event-driven* simulator, meaning that device values are recalculated only when an input change occurs. Thus, the
speed at which the simulation occurs does not depend on delay or
other time values in the circuit.

Primitive Devices

◆ Click on the inverter (NOT) device with the arrow tool in order to select it.

◆ Select the Simulation Params command in the Simulation menu. The following window will appear:

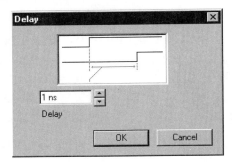

The inverter is classified as a *primitive* device, since its simulation function is built into the program. Primitive devices have a single time value that defines the delay from any input pin to any output pin for any transition. More complex models can be implemented by using pin delays or by building subcircuit devices out of the existing primitives.

◆ Click in the delay value box, and change the number to 5 ns; then click on the OK button. Notice the effect this delay change has on the period of the oscillation in this circuit, as displayed in the timing diagram.

Power and Ground Signals

◆ Select a 74_161 4-bit counter device from the 7400 library, and place it in the circuit diagram as shown.

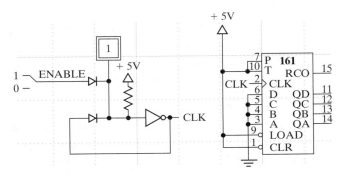

◆ Using the text tool, as described previously, add the names "CLK" and "ENABLE".

◆ Place +5V and Ground symbols as shown to permanently fix these signals to high and low levels, respectively.

Subcircuit Devices

◆ Add the names D0 to D3 using the following procedure:

   ■ Name the least significant counter output D0 using the usual technique.

   ■ Hold down the (CTRL) key on the keyboard while you click on each higher pin in turn. Make sure you click only at the very end of the pin. This will automatically place sequential numbers on the lines clicked.

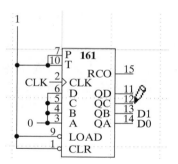

Notice that the traces D0 to D3 in the Timing window will show unknown values, because the counter has never been cleared into a known state.

◆ Press the Clear X (![button]) button in the Simulator toolbar. This resets all storage elements to the zero state and clears unknown lines.

◆ Reactivate the arrow cursor.

◆ Click on the 161 device to select it, and then select the Sim Params command in the Simulation menu.

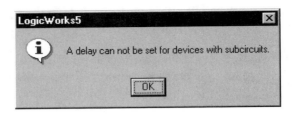

The 161 counter is a *subcircuit device*, meaning that its logic function is implemented using a combination of the LogicWorks primitive devices. Because of this, the overall delay for the device cannot be adjusted by simply changing one parameter. Two methods are available for modifying delays in subcircuit devices and are discussed in the upcoming sections.

◆ Click the OK button on the warning box.

◆ Right-click on the 161 device.

◆ In the pop-up menu, select the Device Info command.

◆ Click on the "Lock Opening Subcircuit" check box to turn it off.

◆ Click on the OK button to close the dialog.

◆ Double-click on the 161 device to open its internal circuit. A new window will open showing the internal circuit of this device, which will appear as follows:

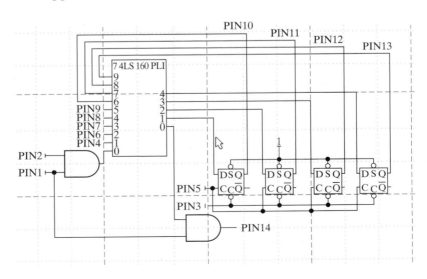

Notice how you can use the Signal Probe tool, the Parameters command, and all the drawing tools to view and modify this internal circuit. If you modify this circuit, *all devices of the same type* in this design will be equally affected.

◆ Close the internal circuit by clicking in the X control at the top right corner of its window.

Pin Delays

◆ Using the arrow cursor, click midway along the QA output pin on the 161 device to select it:

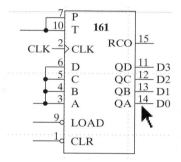

◆ Select the Simulation Params command from the Simulation menu.

LogicWorks allows you to set a delay on an individual pin on a primitive or subcircuit device. The logical effect is the same as if you had inserted a buffer device with the specified delay in series with the pin. Pins always have a default delay of zero.

◆ Set the pin delay to 2 ns and click OK.

Notice the effect this step has on the D0 trace in the Timing window.

Pin delays can be used to customize path delays in subcircuit devices without opening and modifying their internal delays. Setting pin delays on a subcircuit device affects only the single device modified, whereas changing internal delays of primitive devices will affect all copies of the same type of device.

Moving Timing Traces

◆ Click and vertically drag the name CLK in the Timing window to reposition it relative to the other traces:

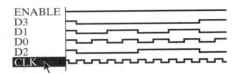

You can reposition any group of traces for ease in making timing comparisons. Any number of traces can be moved at once by holding the (SHIFT) key while clicking on the trace names.

Grouping Timing Traces

◆ Click on the name D0 in the Timing window. Hold the (SHIFT) key down while you click on the names D1, D2, and D3 so that they are all selected.

◆ Click the right mouse button on any of the four selected names.

◆ In the pop-up menu, select the Group command.

You will now see that the four traces D0 to D3 collapse into a single grouped trace showing their combined value in hexadecimal:

The same pop-up menu can be used to ungroup the signals again or to set the signal order used to create the hexadecimal value.

Note that the grouped trace has double vertical bars on some values. This is due to the delay we inserted in the QA output pin. If you set the pin delay back to zero, the double bars will revert back to single bars.

NOTE: The hexadecimal value of a grouped signal will be displayed only if there is sufficient space between the signal changes to display the text. You can use the Zoom In and Zoom Out buttons (◇ ✕) to change the scale factor in order to see the values.

Using the Trigger

◆ Click on the Trigger button (🔫) in the Simulator toolbar.

The trigger mechanism allows you to detect various timing and signal-state conditions.

◆ Type the name CLK in the Names box.

◆ Type the value 1 in the Value box.

◆ Select the Reference Line option. The dialog should now appear as follows:

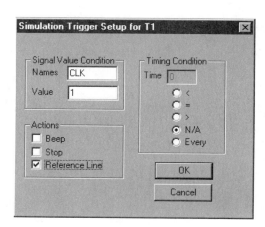

◆ Click the OK button.

You will now see that a reference line is drawn on the Timing window each time the CLK signal changes to a 1 state. You can also enter ranges of signal names (e.g., D7..0) and corresponding hexadecimal values (e.g., 7A) into these boxes in order to match more complex events.

This completes the tutorial section on structural simulation.

7

Tutorial–Using VHDL in LogicWorks

In this tutorial section, we'll look at how you can use the VHDL language to create design descriptions and simulation models. Logic-Works allows you to create designs containing a mix of structural components (that is, schematic diagrams) and VHDL. The topics in this tutorial will get you started in creating each of these types of simulations and tying them together.

◆ For an introduction to the VHDL language, see "Simulation of Digital Systems Using VHDL," on page 87.

Creating a Simple VHDL Simulation

In this section, we create a simple, self-contained VHDL simulation from scratch.

Creating a New VHDL Model

◆ Go to the File menu and select the New command.

◆ In the list of available document types, select Model Wizard and then click OK.

The Model Wizard allows you to create either an independent, top-level design file or a component that can be used inside other designs. Any model can be created using either VHDL or a schematic circuit diagram.

The first panel of the Model Wizard looks like this:

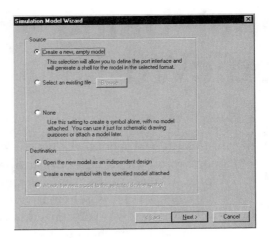

◆ In the Source selections, choose "Create a new, empty model."

◆ In the Destination selections, choose "Open the new model as an independent design."

With these selections, we are essentially creating a new, independent circuit. That is, it will not at this stage be used as a description of a component used in another design.

◆ Click the Next button.

The next pane allows you to choose which type of model you wish to create. In this case, we're going to use VHDL to create a simple AND gate with one inverted input that would look like this in an equivalent logic diagram:

◆ Select VHDL.

◆ Enter a name for the new model, such as AND1INV.

NOTE: Since this name will be used in the VHDL source file, you cannot use a VHDL reserved keyword or anything containing invalid characters as a name. For example, AND would not be a valid name.

◆ Click the Next button.

We now specify the "interface" to the model, that is, what its inputs and outputs will be. In this case, we wish to add two single-bit inputs and one single-bit output. To do this, we proceed as follows:

◆ Set the function to Input, if it is not already.

◆ Enter the name POS for the first input. The note above about names in VHDL applies also to input and output names, so you have to be sure to use something that isn't a reserved word.

◆ Click the Add Single Bit button.

◆ Enter the name NEG, and click the Add Single Bit button again to add the second input.

◆ Go back to the top of the panel and change the Function selection to Output.

◆ Enter the name OUT1, and click the Add Single Bit button.

The port list should now look like this:

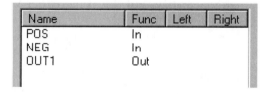

IMPORTANT: The settings in the Func column must appear as shown above!

◆ Click the Finish button to create the model file.

You should now see a new document window open containing text like this:

```
library IEEE;
use IEEE.std_logic_1164.all;

entity AND1INV is

port(
        POS: in        std_logic;
        NEG: in        std_logic;
        OUT1: out      std_logic
    );

end AND1INV;

architecture arch1 of AND1INV is

begin

  -- Your VHDL code defining the model goes here

end arch1;
```

We now have a complete VHDL description of a component having the desired inputs and outputs, except that no code has been added to describe the actual behavior of the device. Before we proceed, we must verify that this is a correct VHDL file.

◆   Go to the VHDL menu and select the Compile command.

You will notice that a new panel appears at the bottom of the screen with the compilation results. You should receive a warning that output OUT1 has not been assigned.

◆   Locate the line that starts _ _ Your VHDL code, and replace it with the following signal assignment statement:

```
OUT1 <= POS AND NOT NEG AFTER 1NS;
```

Running the Simulation

◆ Click the Run ( ) button to start the simulator.

You will now see the VHDL text document turn gray to indicate that it cannot be edited while the simulation is running. Now we need a method of feeding inputs into our design and checking the outputs.

◆ Click the I/O Panel ( ) button. This will cause a new panel to be displayed in the results area at the bottom of the screen.

NOTE: If the I/O Panel has already been used, you might need to click the I/O Panel tab in the Results Panel in order to bring it to the top.

◆ Check the selection list at the top of the I/O Panel. If the name IOPanelDefault.htm is not already displayed, click on the list and choose the item ending with IOPanelDefault.htm.

The I/O Panel is actually a special kind of Web page that can be programmed to display simulation results in many different ways. This default display shows the top-level signals in the design being simulated.

◆ Try clicking the 0 controls to set the inputs to an initial zero state and then the **+** controls in the pos and neg lines to change the input values to these two inputs. Note that the circuit obeys the appropriate truth table:

pos	neg	OUT1
0	0	0
0	1	0
1	0	1
1	1	0

Displaying Timing Results

The I/O Panel is a quick way of viewing circuit inputs and outputs, but gives you no information about the relative timing of signal changes. To view the signals over timing, we will use the Timing window.

◆ Click on the Timing (芷) button to display the timing diagram.

Since the timing diagram was actually collecting results while you were using the I/O Panel, it will display the changes that have occurred up to now:

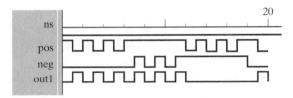

◆ If necessary, you can use the Zoom In and Out (◇ ✕) buttons to adjust the resolution of the timing diagram to get a clear display.

Normally, results windows all share the same panel at the bottom of the screen. If you wish to view the Timing and I/O Panel windows at the same time, proceed as follows:

◆ Click on the I/O Panel tab to bring it to the front.

◆ Click the right mouse button on the I/O Panel tab, and select the Float Current Tab command:

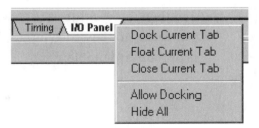

This command places the I/O Panel in a separate, floating window so that you can view both at the same time. You could also have done this to the Timing tab, if desired.

◆ Now try changing the input values again, and watch the effect in the timing diagram.

Note that there is a 1-ns delay between input changes and the corresponding output change. This delay is due to the AFTER 1 NS specification in the VHDL model.

Creating a VHDL Model for a Device Symbol

We'll now look at how we can use VHDL to describe the operation of a device that is going to be used in a LogicWorks circuit diagram. We'll also take the opportunity to use *vectors*, or multibit signals.

◆ First, close any open circuit diagrams or VHDL files.

◆ Select the New command in the File menu, and then double-click on the Model Wizard selection.

◆ For the Source selection, choose "Create a new, empty model."

◆ For the Destination selection, choose "Create a new symbol with the specified model attached." The dialog box should now appear as follows:

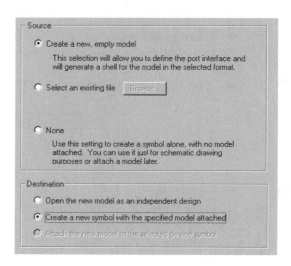

◆ Click the Next button.

◆ Select the VHDL model type, and enter a name, such as COUNT8, for the 8-bit counter device we are going to create:

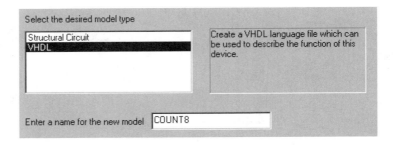

◆ Click the Next button to view the Port Interface panel.

◆ Set the Function to Input, if it isn't already.

◆ Enter the name DIN into the name box.

◆ Enter the number 7 as the Left Bit Number and 0 as the Right Bit Number. Click the Add Vector button. This creates an 8-bit vector with bits numbered from 7 down to 0.

◆ Change the name to CLK, and click the Add Single Bit button.

◆ Change the name to LOAD, and click the Add Single Bit button.

◆ Change the name to DOUT, set the Function to Output, and click the Add Vector button.

◆ You should now see a port list like this:

Name	Func	Left	Right
DIN	In	7	0
CLK	In		
LOAD	In		
DOUT	Out	7	0

◆ Verify that all the port settings are correct, and then click the Next button.

The next panel allows you to specify where the pins will appear on the schematic symbol. By default, inputs will be placed on the left and outputs on the right, which should make sense for most applications. The panel appears as follows:

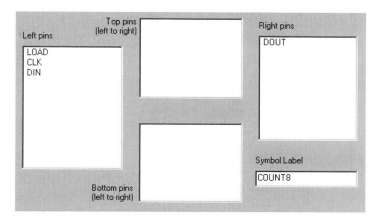

◆ If desired, move the pins to different locations on the symbol by dragging and dropping names from one box to another.

◆ Once you are satisfied with the pin locations, click the Next button.

The last panel allows you to choose the library into which you want to save the new symbol.

◆ If you already have a work library open in the list, you can select it now.

NOTE: We do not recommend saving your own components into the libraries supplied with LogicWorks. Future upgrades to the software might replace those libraries, and you could lose your work.

◆ If you do not have a work library open, use the Open Lib button to open an existing library, or the New Lib button to create a new one.

◆ Once you have selected a library, click the Finish button. A standard Save As box will appear asking you to save the VHDL model file. This step is necessary because the name of the file will be stored with the component.

◆ Save the COUNT8 model file in the default location, or find any suitable folder for it:

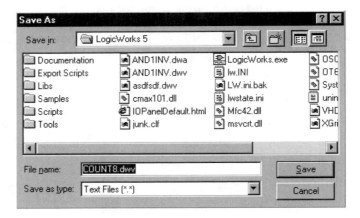

The Model Wizard has now created a VHDL model file that describes all the inputs and outputs, but has no actual behavior. It has also created a device symbol with entries linking it to the file. We now have two steps left: first to fill in the actual behavioral part of the VHDL model, and then to build a test circuit to make sure it works.

◆ Select the New command in the File menu; then choose the Circuit item. This will create a new, empty circuit window on the screen.

◆ Locate the COUNT8 part in the parts list on the right hand side of the screen, and place one of these parts in the circuit. In case you're not familiar with this procedure, refer back to "Placing a Device," on page 22. You should now be looking at a circuit like this:

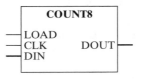

◆ Double-click on the COUNT8 device. This will open the VHDL model in a new window.

◆ After the line "use IEEE.std_logic_1164.all," insert the following additional use statement:

use IEEE.numeric_std.all;

This line is needed because we will be using some arithmetic data types and operations that are defined in this package.

◆ Locate the line near the end of the file that says something like -- Your VHDL code defining the model goes here. (Remember that -- indicates a comment in VHDL.) We are going to replace this line with some code that defines the operation of an 8-bit counter, as follows:

```
clk_proc : process(CLK)
    variable COUNT : unsigned(7 downto 0) := "00000000";
begin
    if CLK'EVENT AND CLK = '1' then
     if LOAD = '1' then
        COUNT := DIN;
     else COUNT := COUNT + 1;
     end if;
    end if;
    DOUT <= COUNT after 500ps;
end process clk_proc;
```

NOTE: Take care when entering the fourth line in the preceding code. The item CLK'EVENT consists of the name CLK followed by an apostrophe (single quote) followed by the word EVENT. For more information on this VHDL attribute, see "Positive-Edge-Triggered D Flip-Flop," on page 149.

◆ Just to make sure you haven't made any errors in the code, go to the VHDL menu and select the Compile command. You should get a message in the VHDL console window at the bottom of the screen indicating that the file compiled without errors. If any errors come up, fix them before proceeding. Here are some things you might want to check:

■ The input and output names (such as CLK) must exactly match the declarations at the top of the file. If you didn't enter the names exactly the same way in the Wizard, the code won't compile correctly.

- ■ VHDL is very fussy about the positions of punctuation such as quote marks and semicolons. Make sure that all the punctuation is entered correctly.

- ■ =, <=, and := can all be read as "equals" to us, but they have very different meanings! Make sure that all instances of these sequences are entered properly.

◆ Once the file compiles correctly, close the COUNT8 document window. You should now be again looking at the circuit containing the COUNT8 symbol. The system description is now complete, so we just have to test it.

Although we could use the I/O Panel as we did in the previous tutorial, we'll take a different approach this time and add circuitry to the diagram in order to test the new device.

◆ Click and hold at the end of the DOUT pin, and extend the bus line as shown:

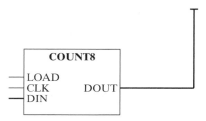

◆ Right-click anywhere along the bus line, and select the Breakout command. This will display the following box:

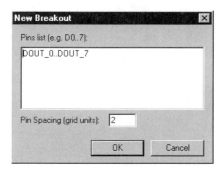

◆ This box should already show the signal range DOUT_0..DOUT_7, which means that all the individual bits from 0 to 7 will be split out of the bus. Click the OK button.

◆ Place the breakout symbol so that it connects to the DOUT bus as shown here:

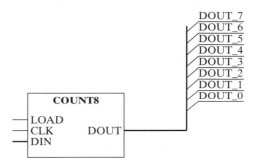

◆ Next locate the Hex Display device in the parts list, and place one so that it connects to the bottom four pins on the breakout. Repeat this step to place a second Hex Display device for the top four pins. The circuit diagram should now appear as follows:

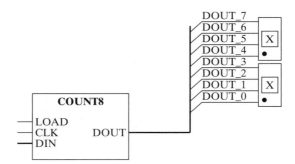

◆ Using a similar procedure, extend the DIN bus to the left, right-click on it to select the Breakout command, and place the break-out. You may need to use the arrow keys on the keyboard to orient the symbol as shown in the next diagram.

◆ Locate the Hex Keyboard device in the parts list. Double-click on it, and move it into the circuit area. You may need to use the arrow keys on the keyboard to orient it the right way to attach to the breakout. Place two keyboards so they connect to the input pins, as shown.

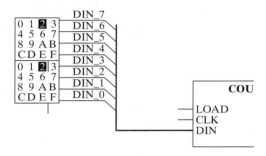

◆ Place a Binary Switch device and wire it to the LOAD input; then place a Clock device and connect it to the CLK pin. You should now have a diagram like this:

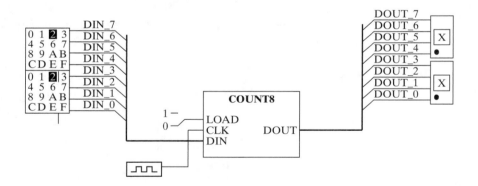

◆ To make it easier to display the results, let's apply names to a couple of the signals that we will want to observe. Select the Text (**A**) tool, and then click on the bus line coming out of the DOUT pin. Enter the name DOUT, and press Enter on the keyboard. Use the same procedure to apply the name CLK to the output of the Clock device. You may want to move some of the devices around to make room for the names.

Here is our final circuit:

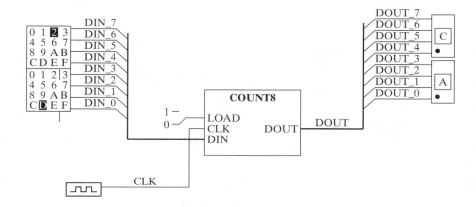

◆ This would be a good time to save this design, in case we want to come back to it later. Select the Save As command in the File menu, and save the design as COUNT8 test or any other name that suits you.

◆ If it is not checked already, select the Show Values command in the Simulation menu in order to show the values of the signal on the circuit diagram.

◆ Click the Run () button to start the simulator.

You should now see the signal value displays change and the time indicator in the toolbar start to advance. Time is advancing because of the Clock device we placed in the circuit. This device generates a continuous sequence of 0-to-1 value changes at its output, regardless of what else is happening in the circuit.

◆ Click on the LOAD switch to change its value to 1.

◆ Click on the hex keypads at the inputs, and observe that the input values are being transferred to the output on the clock.

◆ If it is not already displayed, show the timing diagram by clicking on the Show Timing ( ) button or by clicking on its tab in the results window. If desired, you can change the resolution of the timing diagram by using the Zoom In and Out ( ) tools.

Using a LogicWorks Symbol in a VHDL Design

In this tutorial, we will create a design by using VHDL to create the top-level description and having it refer to LogicWorks symbols as building blocks. This is the reverse of the situation described in the previous tutorial.

IMPORTANT: The VHDL language has more severe restrictions on names than the general LogicWorks program. In order for a symbol to be usable as a device model within a VHDL description, the name of the library itself, the name of the symbol, and the names of all pins on the symbol must meet VHDL naming requirements. In general, this means that names cannot contain any spaces or special characters. Most of the libraries provided with LogicWorks do not meet these requirements, so you must either use the specific libraries provided for this purpose or create your own versions of libraries that have appropriate names.

◆ Select the New command in the File menu, and double-click on the Model Wizard item.

◆ In the Source selections, choose "Create a new, empty model."

◆ In the Destination selections, choose "Open the new model as an independent design."

◆ Click the Next button.

◆ Select the VHDL model type.

◆ Enter the name FULL_ADDER for the new model.

◆ Click the Next button.

We now specify the "interface" to the model, that is, what its inputs and outputs will be. In this case, we wish to add three single-bit inputs and two single-bit outputs. To do this, we proceed as follows:

◆ Set the function to Input, if it is not already.

◆ Enter the name c_in for the first input, and click the Add Single Bit button.

◆ Repeat the foregoing step for inputs named a and b.

◆ Go back to the top of the panel and change the Function selection to Output.

◆ Add output bits sum and c_out.

The port list should now look like this:

Name	Func	Left	Right
c_in	In		
a	In		
b	In		
sum	Out		
c_out	Out		

◆ Click the Finish button to create the model file.

You should now see a new document window open containing text like this:

```
library IEEE;
use IEEE.std_logic_1164.all;

entity full_adder is

port(
        c_in : in   std_logic;
        a     : in   std_logic;
        b     : in   std_logic;
        sum : out std_logic;
        c_out: outstd_logic
    );

end full_adder;

architecture arch1 of full_adder is

begin

  -- Your VHDL code defining the model goes here

end arch1;
```

To make this code into a complete description, we will add component instantiation statements that refer to LogicWorks gate symbols stored in libraries.

◆   In the VHDL file, locate the use statement close to the top of the file. After this line, insert the following additional statements:

```
library Libs;
use Libs.VHDLPrims.all;
```

These statements tell VHDL where to find the components to which we will be referring. The name, in this case VHDLPrims, must refer to a library that is already open in the LogicWorks parts palette.

◆   Locate the architecture statement in the file. On the next line, insert the following declaration:

```
signal s1, s2, s3 : std_logic;
```

This line creates some intermediate signals that will be part of our model.

◆   Find the comment line starting with -- Your VHDL code that appears near the end of the file. Replace this comment with the following lines:

```
G1 : xor_3 port map(INA => c_in, INB => a, INC => b, Y => sum);
G2 : and_2 port map(INA => c_in, INB => a, Y => s1);
G3 : and_2 port map(INA => a, INB => b, Y => s2);
G4 : and_2 port map(INA => c_in, INB => b, Y => s3);
G5 : or_3 port map(INA => s1, INB => s2, INC => s3, Y => c_out);
```

The xor_3, and_2, and or_3 components are all items that will be fetched from the LogicWorks library VHDLPrims. The component names and pin names must exactly match those defined on the symbol.

◆   Use the Save or Save As command to save your file for safekeeping.

◆   Click the Run (⚡) button to start the simulator. If any compilation errors occur, they will be reported in the VHDL console window; otherwise, the VHDL window will go gray to indicate that it is locked while the simulation is running.

◆ Click the I/O Panel (⬚) button. This will display a new panel in the results area at the bottom of the screen.

◆ Try entering values for the a, b, and c_in inputs, and verify that the model is working as expected. Here is the truth table for a full adder that our model should follow:

a	b	c_in	sum	c_out
0	0	0	0	0
0	0	1	1	0
0	1	0	1	0
0	1	1	0	1
1	0	0	1	0
1	0	1	0	1
1	1	0	0	1
1	1	1	1	1

NOTE: The delay values used by the LogicWorks symbols are determined by settings that were applied when the symbols were created. There is no way of changing the delays in the symbols themselves from the VHDL file, although you could apply additional delays to the signals.

8

Tutorial–Creating Device Symbols

This tutorial will show you how to use the symbol editor tool to create your own device symbols.

Creating a New Library

◆ Using the right mouse button, click on the Parts Palette. Select the New Lib command in the pop-up menu.

◆ Create a new library called mylib.clf in the LogicWorks directory or any other convenient location.

Symbol library files hold collections of device symbols along with associated pin function information, default attribute values, and internal-circuit definitions. A single library can contain from one to thousands of part definitions, as suits your application.

Creating a Device Symbol

◆ Click on the New Document ( ) button in the toolbar. Then select Device Symbol and click the OK button. A new device symbol editor window and the associated toolbars will appear:

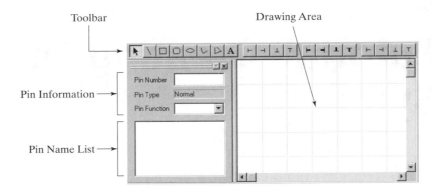

The symbol editor window contains a drawing area for your symbol, plus a toolbar and a Pin Name List. The toolbar includes standard drawing tools as well as special items for normal and bus pin placement.

Setting Pin Name Visibility

By default, the symbol editor displays the name of each pin next to the pin stub. For this example, we want to turn this off. To do this:

◆ Make sure no graphic items are selected in the drawing area, and then select the Properties command in the Objects menu.

◆ Click on the Pin tab, and turn off the Visible switch in the Pin Name area.

◆ Click the OK button.

Setting items in the Properties command with no objects selected sets the default properties when future objects are created.

Drawing the Symbol

◆ Click on the polygon (⌄) tool in the toolbar.

◆ Draw a symbol similar to the one shown in the next diagram by clicking once at each corner point and then double-clicking to terminate the polygon.

The position of the symbol in this window is not important.

Placing Pins

◆ Select the pin (─|) tool.

◆ Place input pins on the symbol by clicking at the positions shown in the next diagram.

◆ Select the pin (|─) tool again.

◆ Place an output pin as shown:

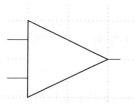

NOTE: The crossbar portion of the pin tool appears only during placement and dragging, for alignment purposes.

Entering Pin Names and Numbers

Placing the pin graphics on the symbol causes pin names to be added automatically to the pin list. In this section, we will enter more meaningful names and add pin numbers.

◆ Double-click on the PIN1 item in the pin list. This will open the name for editing.

◆ Type the new name INA, and then press the Enter key.

◆ Click in the Pin Number box and type 2:

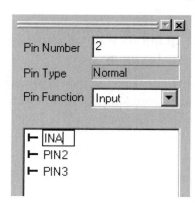

◆ Similarly, select the PIN2 item, enter pin number 3, and change the name to INB.

◆ Select the PIN3 item, enter pin number 6, and change the name to OUT. For this pin only, also change the Pin Function setting to Output.

We have now entered default values for the pin numbers that will appear in a netlist. These values can be edited on the schematic for individual pins, if desired.

Saving and Using the Part

◆ Select the Save command in the File menu.

◆ Enter the part name LM741 or any other desired name.

◆ Double-click on the mylib.clf library in the list in order to select the destination:

◆ Close the symbol editor window.

◆ If mylib.clf library is not already selected, select it in the library drop-down list in the Parts Palette.

◆ Drag the newly created part, and place a copy of it in the schematic. The result should appear as follows:

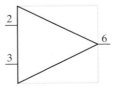

Autocreating a Symbol

For standard types of rectangular symbols, the Autocreate feature will generate a symbol for you in seconds.

◆ Click on the New Document (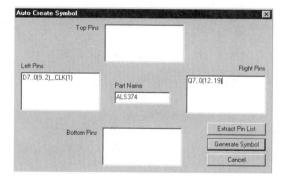) button in the toolbar, and then double-click on Device Symbol.

◆ Select the Auto Create Symbol command in the Options menu.

◆ Make sure that the Show Pin Names on Symbol switch is on.

◆ In the Left Pins box, type the text D7..0(9..2),,,CLK(1):

The entry D7..0 will generate a set of eight pins named D7, D6, etc. (9..2) refers to the corresponding pin numbers. The three commas indicate that we want extra space between these pins. Finally, CLK(1) creates a single pin called CLK with pin number 1. The pin numbers can be omitted, if desired.

◆ In the Right Pins box, type the text Q7..0(12..19).

◆ In the Name box in the center, type ALS374, or any other desired symbol name.

◆ If it is not already, turn on the Show Pin Names on Symbol switch.

◆ Click the Generate button.

The autogenerated symbol should now display the pins and pin numbers entered previously:

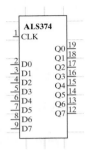

These items can be edited using the drawing tools and Pin Info box, if desired.

◆   Save the new part to the mylib.clf library as described earlier.

◆   Close the symbol editor window.

The symbol can now be placed in a schematic in the usual manner.

Part II
The VHDL Language

9
Simulation of Digital Systems Using VHDL

VHDL programs are unlike programs written in Basic, C++, or Fortran. Conventional programs are based on thinking in terms of algorithms and sequences of calculations that manipulate data toward a specific computational goal. The thought process that goes into writing such programs is inherently procedural, a direct result of the serial nature of most modern computers. Writing VHDL programs is very different. We are not interested so much in the computation of a function, but in mimicking the behavior of some physical system such as a digital circuit. Therefore, the VHDL program must describe this physical system. An associated simulator uses this description and executes a simulation that behaves like the physical system. This chapter discusses the significant structural, physical, and behavioral characteristics of digital systems. It is these characteristics that VHDL programs describe.

Physical systems such as digital circuits do not necessarily behave like procedures. They are characterized by complex interactions between constituent components. In fact, in many cases, the reason we want to simulate a physical system is that we cannot compute what we need to know. For example, if we need to know the average time that a person must wait at a bus stop, we cannot obtain some mathematical function that will compute this value for us. Traffic patterns, whimsical pedestrians, and riders with incorrect change all contribute to a degree of unpredictability and complexity that prevents us from writing a mathematical expression for the waiting time at a bus stop. However, we can simulate the transit system and observe how long people wait in the simulation. If our simulation is accurate, then we will be able to predict reliably the delays that will occur in practice. The digital systems that we will consider do not exhibit probabilistic or random behavior, but are composed of many constituent subsystems and can be quite complex.

In the context of the design of digital systems, there are several compelling reasons for simulation. We may wish to simulate a design prior to implementation in order to ensure that the system meets its specification. For example, we may design a board-level product that interfaces to a camera and processes images in real time. A VHDL simulation of the board may be used to establish that the design can indeed operate fast enough to keep up with the rate at which images are being received from the camera. Given the cost of modern fabrication facilities and the increasing complexity of digital systems, it has become necessary to be able to rely on accurate simulation models to design and test chips and systems prior to their construction. How can we be sure that the design will function as intended or that the design is indeed correct? The VHDL simulation serves as a basis for testing complex designs and validating the design prior to fabrication. The overall effect is that redesign is reduced, the design cycle is shortened, and the product is brought to market sooner.

The features of a language for describing digital systems and the behavior of the simulation itself are quite different from procedural languages. While early simulators for digital systems were written in C and Basic, the developers had to provide new functions, operations, and data types to enable the writing of simulation applications. The definition of the VHDL language, on the other hand, provides a range of features in support of the simulation of digital systems.

As a result of the motivation to model digital systems, many of the concepts and constructs of VHDL can be identified with the structural, behavioral, and physical characteristics of digital systems. We learn best when we can identify with concepts with which we are already familiar. In this chapter, we will review the operational characteristics of digital systems and identify several key attributes. A discrete event model of the operation of a digital system is described that can be utilized to model these attributes and therefore is used for the simulation of digital circuits described in VHDL. We can think of a VHDL program as the description of a digital system; the associated simulator will use this description to produce behavior that will mimic that of the physical system.

Describing Systems

We are interested in being able to describe digital systems at any one of several levels of abstraction, from the switched-transistor level to the computing-system level. To do so requires us to identify attributes of systems common to all of these levels of abstraction. For example, imagine that you are in the business of selling sound cards for personal computers. You are trying to convince Personal Computer, Inc., to include your sound card as a part of its product line by making it available in all of its personal computers. A sample design of your card might appear as shown in Figure 9-1. In order to make this sale, you must be able to describe this card to the engineers of Personal Computer, Inc. How could you describe such a card? What do the engineers need to know in order to evaluate your design? They certainly need to understand the *interface* to the card. For example, what can you connect to this card? Speakers, microphones, or even a stereo amplifier? How does the processor communicate with this card? You must be able to describe all of the signals that may pass through the card interface. The second component of this description is the behavior of the card itself. This description could be communicated in one of several ways. One way is to describe component chips and their interconnection, assuming that the engineers are familiar with the operation of the individual chips. Such a description is commonly referred to as a *structural* description and can be easily conveyed in a block diagram. Alternatively, we can describe the behavior of the card in terms of the type of processing it performs on the input signals and the type of output signals it produces—for example, audio output for the speakers. Such descriptions are referred to as *behavioral* descriptions. You are describing what the card does independently of the physical parts that make up the card. Depending upon who you are talking to, one description or the other is preferable. For example, the marketing department would be interested in the latter description, while the engineering department would be interested in the former.

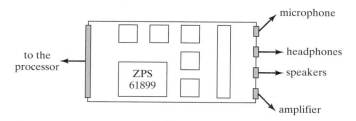

FIGURE 9-1 An example of a system: a sound card.

Structure and behavior are complementary ways of describing systems. The specification of the behavior does not necessarily tell you anything about the structure of the system or the components used to build it. In fact, there are usually many different ways in which you can build a system to provide the same behavior. In such cases, other elements, such as cost or reliability, become the determining factors in choosing the best design. We would expect that any language for describing digital systems will support both structural and behavioral descriptions. We would also expect that the language would enable us to evaluate or simulate several structural realizations of the same behavioral description. The VHDL language provides these features.

Events, Propagation Delays, and Concurrency

Let us look a little closer at these structural and behavioral descriptions. Digital systems are fundamentally about *signals*, specifically binary signals that may take a value of 0 or 1. (A more powerful value system will be introduced later.) Digital circuits are composed of *components* such as gates, flip-flops, and counters. Components are interconnected by wires and transform input signals into output signals. A machine-readable (i.e., programming language) description of a digital circuit must be able to describe the components that make up the circuit, their interconnection, and the behavior of each of the components in terms of their input and output signals and the relation between them. This language description can then be simulated by associated computer-aided design tools.

Consider the gate-level description of the half adder shown in Figure 9-2. There are two input signals, a and b. The circuit computes the value of two output signals, sum and carry. The values of the output signals, sum and carry, are computed as a function of the input signals, a and b. For example, when a = 1 and b = 0, we have sum = 1 and carry = 0. Now, suppose the value of b changes to 1. In this case, say that an *event* occurs on signal b. The event is the change in the value of the input signal from 0 to 1. In our idealized model of the world, this transition takes place instantaneously at a specific, or discrete,

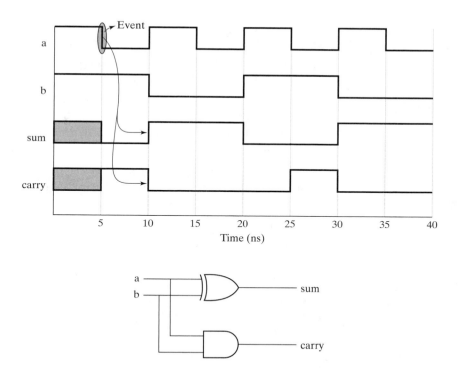

FIGURE 9-2 Half-adder circuit.

point in time. Real circuits take a finite amount of time to switch states, but this approximation is still very useful. From the truth tables for the gates, we know that such an event on b will cause the values of the output signals to change. The signals `sum` and `carry` will acquire values 0 and 1, respectively; that is, events will occur on the signals `sum` and `carry`. We then ask the following basic question: When will these events on the output signals occur relative to the timing of the events on the input signals?

Electrical circuits have a certain amount of inertia, or natural resistance to change. Physical devices such as transistors that are used to implement the gate-level logic take a finite amount of time to switch between logic levels. Therefore, a change in the value of a signal on the input to a gate will not produce an immediate change in the value of the output signal. Rather, it will take a finite amount of time for changes in the inputs to a gate to propagate to the output. This period of time is referred to as the *propagation delay*. The time it takes for changes to propagate through the gates is a function of the physical properties of the gate, including the implementation technology, the design of the gate from basic transistors, and the power supplied to the circuit. From the timing behavior depicted in Figure 9-2, we can see that the gate propagation delay is 5 ns. Electrical currents that carry logic signals through interconnect media such as the wires also travel at a finite rate. Thus, in reality, signals experience propagation delays through wires, and the magnitude of this delay is dependent upon the length of the wire. This delay is nonnegligible, particularly in very high-speed, high-density circuits. It is interesting to note that wires have considerably less inertia than gates. The resulting physical phenomena are therefore quite different for wires and gates. However, as device feature sizes have become increasingly smaller, wire delays have become nonnegligible in modern high-density circuits. As we shall see in later chapters, VHDL provides specific constructs for handling both types of delays. The timing diagram shown in Figure 9-2 does not include wire delays.

A third property of the behavior of the circuit shown in Figure 9-2 is *concurrency* of operation. Once a change is observed on input signal b, the two gates concurrently compute the values of the output signals sum and carry, and new events may subsequently occur on these signals. If both gates exhibit the same propagation delays, then the new events on sum and carry will occur simultaneously. These new events may go on to initiate the computation of other events in other parts of the circuit. For example, consider two half-adders combined to form the full adder shown in Figure 9-3. Events on the input signals In1 or In2 produce events on signals s1 or s3. Events on s1 or s3 in turn may produce events on s2, sum, or c_out. In effect, events on the input signals In1 or In2 propagate to the outputs of the full adder. In the process, many other events internal to the circuit may be generated. In the associated timing diagram, every $0 \rightarrow 1$ and $1 \rightarrow 0$ transition on each signal corresponds to an event. Note the data-driven nature of these systems. Events on signals lead to computations that may generate events on other signals.

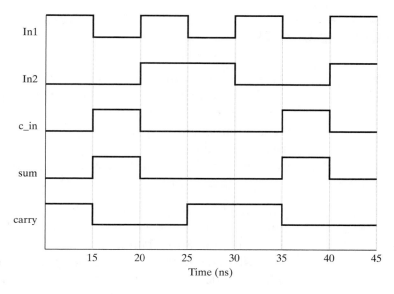

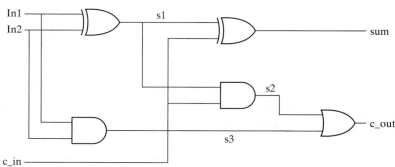

In1	In2	c_in	sum	carry
0	0	0	0	0
0	1	0	1	0
1	0	0	1	0
1	1	0	0	1
0	0	1	1	0
0	1	1	0	1
1	0	1	0	1
1	1	1	1	1

FIGURE 9-3 Full-adder circuit and truth table.

Waveforms and Timing

Over a period of time, the sequence of events that occurs on a signal produces a *waveform* on that signal. The effects of each event may in turn propagate through the circuit, producing waveforms on internal signals and eventually producing waveforms on the output signals. The timing diagram shown in Figure 9-3 is a collection of waveforms on signals in the full-adder circuit, where each waveform is an alternating sequence of $0 \rightarrow 1$ and $1 \rightarrow 0$ transitions or events.

The model of the operation of digital circuits in terms of events, delays, concurrent operation, and waveforms extends to sequential circuits as well as combinational circuits. Consider the operation and timing of the positive-edge-triggered D flip-flop shown in Figure 9-4. The output values are determined at the time of a $0 \rightarrow 1$ transition on the clock signal. At this time, the input value on signal D is sampled and the values of Q and $\overline{Q}$ are determined. Events on the set (S) and reset (R) lines produce events on the output, independent of events on the clock. The unique aspect of the behavior of this model is the dependency on the clock signal. Computation of output events is initiated at a specific point in time, determined by a $0 \rightarrow 1$ event on the Clk signal and independent of events occurring on the D input signal. This need to *wait for* a specific event is an important aspect of the behavior of sequential digital circuits. Such circuits are referred to as *synchronous* circuits. Synchronous circuits operate with a periodic signal commonly referred to as a clock that serves as a common time base. Clocks are an important aspect of digital circuits and deserve special attention.

Alternatively, many digital systems operate asynchronously with request–acknowledge protocols. Operations of these systems are also characterized by the need to *wait* for specific events, such as a request line being asserted.

Signal Values

Signal values are normally associated with the outputs of gates. Wires transfer these values to the inputs of other gates, which, as a result,

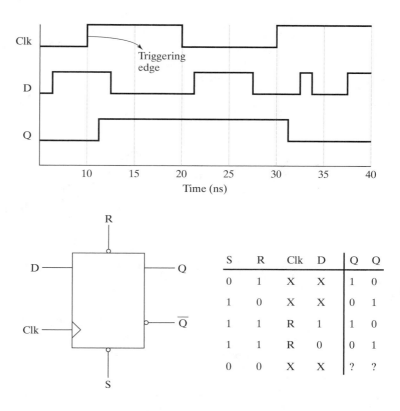

FIGURE 9-4 Excitation table for a positive-edge-triggered D flip-flop (R = rising edge and X = don't care).

may drive their outputs to new values. In general, we tend to think of signals in digital circuits as being binary valued and being driven to these values by a source such as the power supply or the output of a gate. These logical values are physically realized within a circuit by associating logical 0 or 1 values to voltage or current levels at the output of a device. For example, in some circuits, a voltage occurring between 0 and 0.8 volts is recognized as a logical 0 signal, while a voltage occurring in the range 2.0 to 5.0 volts is recognized as logical 1 signal. However, what happens when a signal is not driven to any value—for example, if it is disconnected? What is the value of the signal? It is neither 0 or 1. Such a state is referred to as the high-impedance state and is usually denoted by z. This is a normal, inactive condition and occurs when a signal is (temporarily) disconnected.

What happens when a signal is concurrently driven to both a 0 and a 1 value? This is clearly an abnormal or error condition and should not occur. It is indicative of a design error. How do we denote the value of the signal in such cases? Remember that our overall goal is the accurate description and simulation of digital systems, often for the purpose of testing a design to ensure that it is correct. If this condition were to occur during the simulation of a circuit, the simulator must be able to represent the value of the signal and propagate the effects of this design error through the circuit. Such unknown values are typically denoted by x. What if the initial value of a signal is undefined? How can we represent this value and propagate the effects of uninitialized signal values in order to determine the effect on the operation of the circuit? Such values are typically denoted by u.

At the very least, we see that 0 and 1 values alone are insufficient to accurately capture the behavior of digital systems. We will see that the VHDL language is flexible enough to enable the definition of a range of values for signals. Early in the evolution of VHDL, CAD tool vendors defined their own value systems. Some vendors even had as many as 46 distinct values for a binary signal! This factor made it difficult to share VHDL models. Imagine if different C compilers had different definitions of the values of integers. The same C program could then produce different results, depending upon the compilers that were used. In addition to 0, 1, z, x, and u values, it is useful to denote the concept of *signal strength*. The strength of a signal reflects the ability of the source device to supply energy to drive the signal. This strength can be weakened or attenuated by, for example, the resistance of the wires, giving rise to signals of different strengths. Although the range of strength values can be large, only two levels are sufficient to characterize certain types of transistor circuits. The use of strength values facilitates certain styles of design. The VHDL language is being widely used to describe the behavior of circuits that can be automatically synthesized by design tools. A value system that incorporates the concept of signal strength is therefore necessary.

In an attempt to establish common ground and enable the construction of portable models, the Institute of Electrical and Electronics Engineers (IEEE) has approved a nine-value system. This system is the IEEE 1164 standard and is rapidly gaining acceptance

Value	Interpretation
U	Uninitialized
X	Forcing Unknown
0	Forcing 0
1	Forcing 1
Z	High Impedance
W	Weak Unknown
L	Weak 0
H	Weak 1
-	Don't Care

FIGURE 9-5 IEEE 1164 value system.

and widespread usage. In this system, binary signals take on functional values of 0 or 1. However, they can also be unknown (x), uninitialized (u), or not driven (z). If we include two levels of signal strength and the don't-care value (-), we have the IEEE 1164 value system, shown in Figure 9-5. It is important to note that this value system is not a part of the VHDL language, but rather a standard definition that vendors are motivated to support and users are motivated to use, since it enables reuse of designs and sharing of models between users. Practically all vendors support the IEEE 1164 value system.

Shared Signals

It is common for components in a digital circuit to have multiple sources for the value of an input signal. However, connecting all sources and destinations by dedicated signal paths can be expensive. Therefore many designs will use *buses*: a group of signals that can be shared among multiple source and destination components. For example, the architecture of personal computers and workstations is built around one or more buses. The microprocessor chip may drive a data bus to communicate values to memory, while, at other times, the memory controller may drive the bus to return values. The Input/Output buses in PCs interconnect many devices such as CD-ROMs, floppy disk drives, and hard disk drives, that can be the source of values on the Input/Output bus, although not at the same time. Certain forms of switching circuits are carefully designed based on *wired logic*. In these circuits, the interconnection of wires can produce AND and OR Boolean functions. For example, if several devices drive a shared signal to either 0 or z, then the signal value will be determined by the interactions among all of the values applied to it. In this case, if at least one device is driving the signal to a 0, the value of the signal will be 0. Thus, the interconnection can be regarded as implementing a wired-OR function.

In general, when multiple drivers exist for a signal, what value does the signal have? Clearly, the answer depends on the implementation. Shared signals such as buses are supposed to have only one active source at any given time, but this is not the case for circuits based on wired logic. A hardware description language must be capable of describing the interactions between multiple drivers for shared signals.

A Discrete-Event Simulation Model

The preceding sections described the behavior of digital systems in terms of events that take place at discrete points in time. Some events may cause other events to be generated after some delay, and many events may be generated concurrently. *Discrete-event simulation* is a programming-based methodology for accurately modeling the generation of events in physical systems. The operation of a physical system such as a digital circuit is described in a computer program that specifies how and when events—changes in signal values—are generated. A *discrete-event simulator* then executes this program, modeling the passage of time and the occurrence of events at various points in time. Such simulators often manage millions of events and rely on well-developed techniques to keep track accurately of the *correct order* in which the events occur. We can view VHDL as a programming language for describing the generation of events in digital systems supported by a discrete-event simulator. This section describes a simple discrete-event simulation model that captures the basic elements of the simulation of VHDL programs. Understanding the VHDL model of time is a necessary prelude to writing, debugging, and understanding VHDL models.

Discrete-event simulations use an event-list data structure. The event list maintains an ordered list of all future events in the circuit. Each event is described by the type of event—a $0 \rightarrow 1$ or $1 \rightarrow 0$ transition—and the time at which it is to occur. Although we generally think of transitions as a change of value from 0 to 1 or vice versa, recall that signals may have other values. In general, an event is simply a change in the value of a signal. Let us refer to the time at which an event is to occur as the *timestamp* of that event. The event list is ordered according to increasing timestamp value. This structure enables the simulator to execute events in the order that they occur in the real world, that is, the physical system. Finally, the simulator clock records the passage of simulated time. The value of this clock will be referred to as the *current timestep*, or simply the timestep. Imagine what would happen if we froze the system at a timestep and took a snapshot of the values of all of the signals in the system. These values would represent the state of the simulation at that point in time.

Let us consider one approach to the discrete-event simulation of the half-adder circuit shown in Figure 9-2. Assume that we have been able to specify waveforms on the inputs a and b. In a physical circuit, these waveforms would likely be generated as the output of another component. At timestep 0 ns, initial values on inputs a and b will cause events that set the values of the sum and carry signals. Assuming that the propagation delay of a gate is 5 ns, these events will be scheduled 5 ns later. Figure 9-6(a) shows these events at the head of the event list at time 5 ns. Note that both sum and carry are scheduled to receive values at this time. Prior to this time, the values of the sum and carry are undefined, as represented by the shaded areas in the timing diagram shown in Figure 9-2. Input a is also scheduled to make a transition at the same time. (For the moment, let us ignore how these events on the input signal are generated.) These events correspond to the signal transitions shown on the timing diagram in Figure 9-2 at 5 ns. The simulator removes these events from the event list, and the current values of these signals are updated. Due to a change in the value of signal a, the simulator determines that the

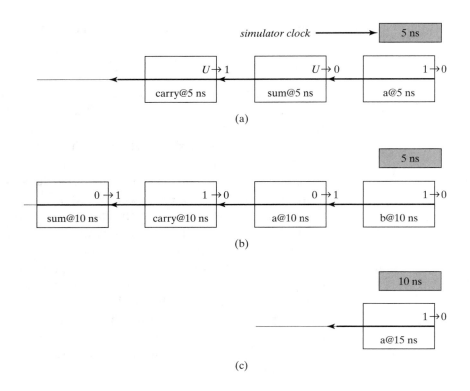

FIGURE 9-6 Discrete-event simulation of the half-adder.

values of the output signals, sum and carry, have to be recomputed. The computation produces new values of sum and carry, which are scheduled in the event list at timestep 10 ns. The head of the event list now appears as shown in Figure 9-6(b), with all of the events scheduled for timestep 10 ns. The global clock is now updated to 10 ns, all events scheduled at timestep 10 ns are removed from the event list, the corresponding signal values are updated, and any new events are computed and scheduled. Figure 9-6(c) shows the head of the event list after event computations at timestep 10 ns, and prior to the update of the global clock. The simulator clock will now be updated to 15 ns and the process repeated. This sequence is continued until there are no more events to be computed or until some predetermined simulation time has expired. This preceding behavior of a discrete-event simulator can be described in the following steps:

1. Advance the simulation time to that of the event with the smallest timestamp in the event list. This is the event at the head of the list.

2. Execute all events at this timestep by updating signal values.

3. Execute the simulation models of all components affected by the new signal values.

4. Schedule any future events.

5. Repeat until either the event list is empty or a preset simulation time has expired.

In general, there is substantial concurrency in a digital circuit, and many events may take place simultaneously. Thus, many signals may receive values at the same timestep, and more than one event is executed at a timestep. We see that the simulator employs a two-stage model of the evolution of time. In the first stage, the simulation time is advanced to that of the next event, and all signals receiving values at this time are updated. In the second stage, all components affected by these signal updates are reevaluated, and any future events that are generated by these evaluations are scheduled by placing them into the event list in order of their timestamp.

It is apparent that this model is quite flexible and general. We can consider using it to model gate-level circuits as well as higher level circuits such as arithmetic logic units (ALUs), decoders, multiplexors, and even microprocessors. We simply need to describe the behavior of these components in terms of input events, computation of the output events from the input events, and propagation delays. If we can describe a digital system in these terms, we can develop computer programs for implementing this behavior. Note that discrete-event simulation itself is only a model of the behavior of real systems. In real circuits, signals do not make instantaneous transitions between logic-0 voltage levels and logic-1 voltage levels. For that matter, there is no such thing as a truly digital device. There are only analog devices wherein we interpret analog voltage levels as 0 or 1! For many purposes, though, our discrete-event model is adequate. However, more detailed and accurate models are often required, in which case complementary techniques and models are employed. To distinguish the discrete-event model from the real system, we will refer to the former as the *logical model* and the latter as the *physical system*.

Chapter Summary

This chapter is based on the premise that we must understand the execution model of the VHDL language before we can use it effectively. The VHDL language was motivated by the need to accurately model and simulate digital systems. This chapter has focused on the attributes of the behavior of digital systems. By identifying these attributes in this chapter and establishing the terminology, it was possible to describe a general discrete-event model for the execution of VHDL programs. Hopefully, this chapter has provided an intuitive basis for the reader to learn and apply the VHDL language constructs described in succeeding chapters. The key attributes discussed in this chapter include:

- System descriptions
  - ◆ structural
  - ◆ behavioral
- Events
- Propagation delays
- Concurrency
- Timing
  - ◆ synchronous
  - ◆ asynchronous
- Waveforms
- Signal values
- Shared signals
- Discrete-event simulation

The VHDL language provides basic constructs for representing each of the above attributes. The associated simulator implements a discrete-event simulation model, manages the progression of simulated time, and maintains internal representations of the waveforms being generated on signals. The language constructs to specify these attributes are described in the following chapters.

10

Basic Language Concepts

VHDL has often been criticized as being overly complex and intimidating to the novice user. While the language is extensive, a quick start towards building useful simulation models can be made by relying on a core set of language constructs. This chapter describes the language constructs provided within VHDL for describing the attributes of digital systems, such as events, propagation delays, concurrency, and waveforms. Chapter 11 then introduces concepts that extend the constructs introduced here in order to enable the application of conventional programming constructs in building models of complex digital systems, particularly at higher levels of abstraction. Collectively, these two chapters provide us with the tools necessary to model all of the attributes of digital systems described in Chapter 9.

Signals

Conventional programming languages manipulate basic objects such as variables and constants. Variables receive values through assignment statements and can be assigned new values through the course of a computation. Constants, on the other hand, may not change their values. In contrast, digital systems are fundamentally about *signals*. We have seen that signals may take on one of several values, such as 0, 1, or z. Signals are analogous to the wires used to connect components of a digital circuit. To capture the behavior of digital signals, the VHDL language introduces a new type of programming object: the `signal` object type. Like variables, signals may be assigned values, but differ from variables in that they have an associated *time value*, since a signal receives a value at a specific point in time. The signal retains this value until it is assigned a new value at a future point in time. The sequence of values assigned to a signal over time is the *waveform* of the signal. It is primarily this association with time–value pairs that differentiates a signal from a variable. A variable always has one current value. At any instant in time, however, a signal may be associated with several time–value pairs, where each time–value pair represents some future value of the signal.

Finally, we note that variables may be declared to be of a specific type, such as **integer** or **character**. In a similar manner, a signal can be declared to be of a specific type. When used in this way, a signal does not necessarily have correspondence with the wires that connect digital components. For example, we may model the output of an ALU as an integer value. This output is treated as a signal and in simulation behaves as a signal by receiving values at specific points in time. However, we do not have to concern ourselves with modeling the number of bits necessary at the output of the ALU. This behavior enables us to model systems at a higher level of abstraction than digital circuits. Such high-level simulation is useful in the early stages of the design process, where many details of the design are still being developed.

Before we can understand how to declare and operate on signals, we must first cover the basic programming constructs in VHDL. We will return to discuss signal objects in greater detail later in this chapter.

Entity–Architecture

We start by addressing the description of digital systems. The primary programming abstraction in VHDL is a *design entity*. Examples of design entities include a chip, a board, and a transistor. A design entity is a component of a design whose behavior is to be described and simulated. Consider once again the gate-level digital circuit for a half-adder, shown again in Figure 10-1. There are two input signals, a and b. The circuit computes the value of two output signals, sum and carry. This half-adder circuit represents an example of a design entity.

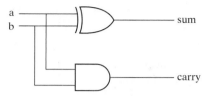

FIGURE 10-1 Half-adder circuit.

How can the half-adder circuit be accurately described? Imagine that you had to describe this circuit over the telephone to a friend who was familiar with digital logic gates, but was not familiar with the half-adder. Your description would most likely include the input signals, the output signals, and a description of the behavior. The behavior, in turn, may be specified with a truth table, Boolean equations, or simply an interconnection between gates. We observe that there are two basic components to the description of any design entity: (i) the interface to the design and (ii) the internal behavior of the design. The VHDL language provides two distinct constructs to specify the interface and internal behavior of design entities, respectively.

The external interface to this entity is specified with the **entity** declaration. For the circuit shown in Figure 10-1, the entity declaration would appear as follows:

```
entity half_adder is
port(a, b: in bit;
       sum, carry: out bit);
end half_adder;
```

The boldface type denotes keywords that are VHDL reserved keywords. The remaining words are user supplied. Just as we name programs, the label `half_adder` is the name given to this design entity by the programmer. Note that the VHDL language is *case insensitive*. The inputs and outputs of the circuit are referred to as *ports*. The ports are special programming objects and are signals. Ports are the means by which the half-adder can communicate with the external world or other circuits. Therefore, naturally, we expect ports to be signals rather than variables. Like variables in conventional programming languages, each port must be a signal that is declared to be of a specific type. In this case, each port is declared to be of type **bit**, and represents a single-bit signal. A **bit** is a signal type that is defined within the VHDL language and can take a value of 0 or 1. A **bit_vector** is a signal type composed of a vector of signals, each of type **bit**. The types **bit** and **bit_vector** are two common types of ports. In general, a port may be one of several other VHDL data types as well. Common data types and operators supported by the language are described in the VHDL reference manual provided in electronic form with the software.

From our study of digital logic, we know that bits and bit vectors are fundamental signals. From previous chapters, we know that, in reality, signals can take on many values other than 0 and 1. Thus, in practice, the types **bit** and **bit_vector** are of limited use. The IEEE 1164 standard is gaining widespread acceptance as a value system. In this standard the nine-value signal would be declared to be of type std_ulogic rather than **bit**. Analogously, we would have the type std_ulogic_vector rather than **bit_vector**. Therefore, throughout the remainder of this text, all examples will utilize the IEEE 1164 standard signal and data types. The preceding entity declaration now appears as follows:

```
entity half_adder is
port(a, b: in std_ulogic;
        sum, carry: out std_ulogic);
end half_adder;
```

The signals appearing in a port declaration may be distinguished as input signals, output signals, or bidirectional signals. This is referred to as the *mode* of the signal. In the above example, the **in** and **out** specifications denote the mode of the signal. Bidirectional signals are of mode **inout**. Every port in the entity description must have its mode and type specified.

We see that it is relatively straightforward to write the entity descriptions of standard digital logic components. The upcoming examples show some sample circuits and their entity descriptions. Note how byte- and wordwide groups of bits are specified. For example, a 32-bit quantity is declared to be of the type std_ulogic_vector (31 **downto** 0). This type refers to a data item that is 32 bits long, where bit 31 is the most significant bit in the word and bit 0 is the least significant bit in the word.

Example: Entity Declaration of a 4-to-1 Multiplexor

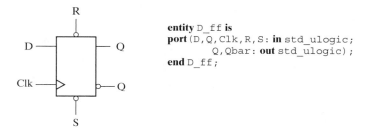

```
entity mux is
port (I0,I1: in std_ulogic_vector(7 downto 0);
         I2,I3   : in std_ulogic_vector(7 downto 0);
         Sel     : in std_ulogic_vector(1 downto 0);
         Z       : out std_ulogic_vector(7 downto 0));
end mux;
```

Example End: Entity Declaration of a 4-to-1 Multiplexor

Example: Entity Declaration of a D Flip-Flop

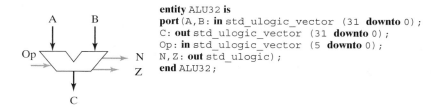

```
entity D_ff is
port(D,Q,Clk,R,S: in std_ulogic;
        Q,Qbar: out std_ulogic);
end D_ff;
```

Example End: Entity Declaration of a D Flip-Flop

Example: Entity Declaration of a 32-Bit ALU

```
entity ALU32 is
port(A,B: in std_ulogic_vector (31 downto 0);
     C: out std_ulogic_vector (31 downto 0);
     Op: in std_ulogic_vector (5 downto 0);
     N,Z: out std_ulogic);
end ALU32;
```

Example End: Entity Declaration of a 32-Bit ALU

From the preceding examples, it is clear that design entities can occur at multiple levels of abstraction, from the gate level to large systems. In fact, it should be apparent that a design entity does not even have to represent digital hardware! The description of the interface is simply a specification of the input and output signals of the design entity.

Once the interface to the digital component or circuit has been described, it is now necessary to describe its internal behavior. The VHDL construct that enables us to specify the behavior of a design entity is the **architecture** construct. The syntax of the architecture construct is as follows:

> **architecture** behavioral **of** half_adder **is**
> -- *place declarations here* --
> **begin**
> -- *place description of behavior here* --
> **end** behavioral;

The above construct provides for the declaration of the module named behavioral, which will contain the description of the behavior of the design entity named half_adder. Such a module is referred to as the *architecture* and is associated with the entity named in the declaration. Thus, the description of a design entity takes the form of an entity–architecture pair. The architecture description is linked to the correct entity description by providing the name of the corresponding entity in the first line of the architecture.

The behavioral description provided in the architecture can take many forms. These forms differ in the levels of detail, the description of events, and the degree of concurrency. The remainder of this chapter focuses on a core set of language constructs required to model the attributes of digital systems described in Chapter 9. Subsequent chapters will add constructs motivated by the need for expanding the scope and level of abstraction of the systems to be modeled.

Concurrent Statements

The operation of digital systems is inherently concurrent. Many components of a circuit can be simultaneously operating and concurrently driving distinct signals to new values. How can we describe the assignment of values to signals? We know that signal values are time–value pairs; that is, a signal is assigned a value by at a specific point in time.

Within VHDL, signals are assigned values by using *signal assignment statements*. These statements specify a new value of a signal and the time at which the signal is to acquire this value. Multiple signal assignment statements are executed concurrently in simulated time and are referred to as *concurrent signal assignment statements* (*CSAs*). There are several forms of CSA statements, and they are described in the following section.

Simple Concurrent Signal Assignment

Consider the following description of the behavior of the half-adder circuit shown in Figure 10-1:

```
architecture concurrent_behavior of half_adder is
begin
  sum <= (a xor b) after 5 ns;
  carry <= (a and b) after 5 ns;
end concurrent_behavior;
```

Recall that, although VHDL manages the progression of time, we need to be able to specify events, delays, and concurrency of operation. Just as we named entity descriptions, the label concurrent_behavior is the name given to this architecture module. The first line denotes the name of the entity that contains the description of the interface of this design entity. Each statement in the above architecture is a signal assignment statement, with the operator <= denoting signal assignment. Each statement describes how the value of the output signal depends on, and is computed from, the value of the input signals. For example, the value of the sum output signal is computed as the Boolean exclusive-OR operation of the two input signals. Once the value of sum has been computed, it will not change unless the value of a or b changes. Figure 10-2 illustrates this behavior. At the current time, a = 0, b = 1, and sum = 1. At time 10, the value of b changes to 0. The new value of the sum will be (a **xor** b) = 0. Since there will be a propagation delay through the exclusive-OR gate, the signal sum will be assigned this value 5 ns later, at time 15. This behavior is captured in the first signal assignment statement. Note that, unlike variable assignment statements, the signal assignments shown above specify both value and (relative) time.

```
library IEEE;
use IEEE.std_logic_1164.all;

entity half_adder is
port ( a,b  : in std_logic;
       sum,carry : out std_logic);
end half_adder;

architecture concurrent_behavior of half_adder is
begin
sum<= (a xor b) after 5 ns;
carry<= (a and b) after 5 ns;
end concurrent_behavior;
```

FIGURE 10-2 Operation of a half-adder.

In general, if an event (signal transition) occurs on a signal on the right-hand side of a signal assignment statement, the expression is evaluated and new values for the output signal are scheduled for some time in the future as defined by the **after** keyword. The dependency of the output signals on the input signals is captured in the two statements and not in the textual order of the program. The order of the statements could be reversed, but the behavior of the circuit would not change. Both statements are executed concurrently with respect to simulated time in order to reflect the concurrency of corresponding operations in the physical system. This is why these statements are referred to as concurrent signal assignment statements. A fundamental difference between VHDL programs and conventional programming languages is that concurrency is a natural part of the systems described in VHDL and therefore of the language itself. Note that the execution of the statements is determined by the flow of signal values, rather than textual order. Figure 10-2 shows a complete, executable half-adder description and the associated timing behavior. This description contains the most common elements used to describe a design entity.

Note the use of the **library** and **use** clauses. We can think of libraries as repositories for frequently used design entities that we wish to share. The **library** clause identifies a library that we wish to access. The name is a logical name for a library. In Figure 10-2, the library name is IEEE. In practice, this logical name will usually map to a directory on the local system. This directory will contain various design units that have been compiled. A *package* is one such design unit. A package may contain definitions of types, functions, or procedures to be shared by multiple application developers. The **use** clause determines which of the packages or other design units in a library you will be using in the current design. In the preceding example, the **use** clause states that in library IEEE, there is a package named std_logic_1164 and that we will be able to use all of the components defined in this package. We need this package, since the definition for the type std_ulogic is in this package. The VHDL models that use the IEEE 1164 value system will include the package declaration as shown. Design tool vendors typically provide the library IEEE and the std_logic_1164 package. These concepts are analogous to the use of libraries for mathematical functions and input/output in conventional programming languages. Libraries and packages are described in greater detail in Chapter 13. This example now contains the major components found in VHDL models: declarations of existing design units in libraries that you will be using, the entity description of the design unit, and the architecture description of the design unit.

The descriptions provided so far in this chapter are based on the specification of the value of the output signals as a function of the input signals. In larger and more complex designs, there are usually many internal signals used to connect design components such as gates or other hardware building blocks. The values that these signals acquire can also be written using simple concurrent signal assignment statements. However, we must be able to declare and make use of signals other than those within the entity description. The gate-level description of the full adder provides an example of such a VHDL model.

Example: Full-Adder Model

Consider the full-adder circuit shown in Figure 10-3. We are interested in an accurate simulation of this circuit in which all of the signal transitions in the physical realization are modeled. In addition to the ports in the entity description, we see that there are three internal signals. These signals are named and declared in the architectural description. The declarative region declares three single-bit signals: s1, s2, and s3. These signals are annotated in the circuit. Now we are ready to describe the behavior of the full adder in terms of the internal signals as well as the entity ports. Since this circuit uses two input gates, each signal is computed as a Boolean function of two other signals. The model is a simple statement of *how* each signal is

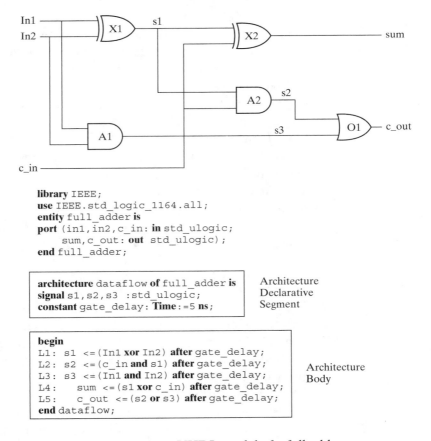

```
library IEEE;
use IEEE.std_logic_1164.all;
entity full_adder is
port (in1,in2,c_in: in std_ulogic;
      sum,c_out: out std_ulogic);
end full_adder;
```

```
architecture dataflow of full_adder is    Architecture
signal s1,s2,s3 :std_ulogic;              Declarative
constant gate_delay: Time:=5 ns;           Segment
```

```
begin
L1:  s1 <=(In1 xor In2) after gate_delay;
L2:  s2 <=(c_in and s1) after gate_delay;      Architecture
L3:  s3 <=(In1 and In2) after gate_delay;      Body
L4:     sum <=(s1 xor c_in) after gate_delay;
L5:     c_out <=(s2 or s3) after gate_delay;
end dataflow;
```

FIGURE 10-3 VHDL model of a full adder.

computed as a function of other signals, as well as the propagation delay through the gate. There are two output signals and three internal signals, for a total of five signals. Accordingly, the description consists of five concurrent signal assignment statements, one for each signal.

Each signal assignment statement is given a label: L1, L2, and so on. This labeling is optional and can be used for reference purposes. Note a new language feature in this model—the use of the **constant** object. Constants in VHDL function in a manner similar to conventional programming languages. A constant can be declared to be of a specific type, in this case of type **Time**. A constant must have a value at the start of the simulation, and that value cannot be changed during the simulation. At this stage, it is easiest to ensure that constants are initialized as shown in Figure 10-3. The introduction of the type **Time** is a natural consequence of simulation modeling. Any object of this type must take on the values of time, such as microseconds or nanoseconds. The type **Time** is a predefined type of the language. As we know, the textual order of the statements is irrelevant to the correct operation of the circuit model.

Let us now consider the flow of signal values and the sequence of execution of the signal assignment statements. Figure 10-4 shows the waveforms of all of the signals in the full-adder circuit. From the

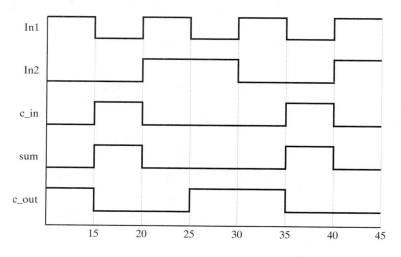

FIGURE 10-4 Full-adder circuit timing.

figure, we see that an event on In1 is changing its value to 1 at time 10. This change causes statements L1 and L3 (from Figure 10-3) to be executed and new values to be scheduled on signals s1 and s3 at time 15. These events in turn cause statements L2 and L5 to be executed at time 20 and events to be scheduled on signals c_out and s2 at time 20. We thus see that the execution of statement L1 produced events that caused the execution of statement L5. This order of execution is maintained regardless of the textual order in which the statements appear in the program.

Note the two-stage model of execution. In the first stage, all statements with events occurring at the current time on signals on the right-hand side (RHS) of the signal assignment statement are evaluated. All future events that are generated from the execution of these statements are then scheduled. Time is now advanced to the time of the next event. The process is then repeated. Note how the programmer specifies events, delays, and concurrency: Events are specified with signal assignment statements. Delays are specified within the signal assignment statement. Concurrency is specified by having a distinct signal assignment statement for each signal. The order of execution of the statements is dependent upon the flow of values (just as is the case in the real circuit) and not on the textual order of the program. As long as the programmer correctly specifies how the value of each signal is computed and when it acquires this value relative to the current time, the simulator will correctly reflect the behavior of the circuit.

Example End: Full-Adder Model

Implementation of Signals

Unlike variables, signals are a new type of programming object and merit specific attention. So far, we have seen that signals can be declared in the body of an architecture or in the port declaration of an entity. The form of the declaration is

    signal s1 : std_ulogic := '0';

or, more generally,

    identifier-list : type := expression;

If the signal declaration includes the assignment symbol (i.e., :=) followed by an expression, then the value of the expression is the initial value of the signal. The initialization is not required, however, in which case the signal is assigned a default value as specified by the type definition. Signals can be one of many valid VHDL types: integers, real, bit_vector, and so forth.

Now consider the assignment of values to a signal. We know that signal assignment statements assign a value to a signal at a specific point in time. The simple concurrent signal assignment statements described so far in this chapter exhibit the common structure

sum <= (a **xor** b) **after** 5 **ns**;

which can be written in a more general form as

signal <= *value expression* **after** *time expression;*

The expression on the right-hand side of the signal assignment statement is referred to as a *waveform element*. A waveform element describes an assignment to a signal and is composed of a *value expression* to the left of the **after** keyword and a *time expression* to the right of that keyword. The former evaluates to the new value to be assigned to the signal, and the latter evaluates to the relative time at which the signal is to acquire this value. In this case, the new value is computed as the exclusive-OR of the current values of the signals a and b. The value of the time expression is added to the current simulation time in order to determine when the signal will receive this new value. In this case, the time expression is a constant value of 5 ns. With respect to the current simulation time, this time–value pair represents the future value of the signal and is referred to as a *transaction*. The underlying discrete-event simulator that executes VHDL programs must keep track of all transactions that occur on a signal. The list is ordered in increasing time of the transactions.

If the evaluation of a single waveform element produces a single transaction on a signal, can we specify multiple waveform elements and, as a result, multiple transactions? For example, could we have the following?

s1 <= (a **xor** b) **after** 5 **ns**, (a or b) **after** 10 **ns**, (**not** a) **after** 15 **ns**;

The answer is yes! When an event occurs on either of the signals a or b, then the above statement will be executed, all three waveform elements will be evaluated, and three transactions will be generated. Note that these transactions are in increasing order of time. The events represented by these transactions must be scheduled at different points in the future, and the VHDL simulator must keep track of all of the transactions that are currently scheduled on a signal. This is achieved by maintaining an ordered list of all of the current transactions pending on a signal. This list is referred to as the *driver* for the signal. The current value of a signal is the value of the transaction at the head of the list.

What is the physical interpretation of such a sequence of events? These events represent the value of the signal over time, which essentially is a waveform. This is how we can represent a signal waveform in VHDL: as a sequence of waveform elements. Therefore, within a signal assignment statement, rather than assigning a single value to the signal at some future time, we can assign a waveform to the signal. This waveform is specified as a sequence of signal values, and each value is specified with a single waveform element. Within the simulator, these sequences of waveform elements are represented as a sequence of transactions on the driver of the signal. These transactions are referred to as the *projected output waveform*, since these events have not yet occurred in the simulation. What if the simulation attempts to add transactions that conflict with the current projected waveform? The VHDL language definition provides specific rules for adding transactions to the projected waveform of a signal.

Example: Specifying Waveforms

Assume that we would like to generate the following waveform:

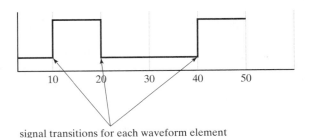

signal transitions for each waveform element

We could do so with the following signal assignment statement:

```
signal <= '0','1' after 10 ns,'0' after 20 ns,'1' after 40 ns;
```

Note how each transition in the foregoing waveform is specified as a single waveform element in the signal assignment statement. All waveform elements must be ordered in terms of increasing time. Failure to do so will result in an error.

Example End: Specifying Waveforms

Note how the concepts and terminology discussed so far are derived from the operation of digital circuits. In a physical circuit, a wire (signal) has a driver associated with it. Over time, this driver produces a waveform on that wire. If we continue to view the language constructs by analogy with the digital circuits they were intended to model, it will be easier for us to reason about the use of VHDL in constructing models. The constructs that manipulate signals invariably rely on waveform elements to specify input and output waveforms. Understanding this representation is key to understanding many of the VHDL programming constructs.

Resolved Signals

Our view of signals up to this point has been one where every signal has only one driver, that is, one signal assignment statement that is responsible for generating the waveform on that signal. However, we know that this view is not true in practice. Shared signals occur on buses and in circuits based on wired logic. When a signal has multiple drivers, how is the value of the signal determined? In the VHDL language, this value is determined by a *resolution function*.

A resolution function examines all of the drivers on a shared signal and determines the value to be assigned to the signal. A shared signal must be of a special type: a *resolved type*. A resolved type has a resolution function associated with the type. In the preceding examples, we used the `std_ulogic` and `std_ulogic_vector` types for single-bit and multibit signals, respectively. The corresponding resolved types are `std_logic` and `std_logic_vector`. This distinction has the following consequences: In the course of the simulation, when a signal of type `std_logic` is assigned a value, the associated resolution function is automatically invoked to determine the correct value of the signal. Multiple drivers for this signal may be projecting multiple future values for this signal. The resolution function examines these drivers in order to return the correct value of the signal at the current time. If the signal has only one driver, then determination of the value is straightforward. However, if more than one driver exists for the signal, then the value that is assigned to the signal is the value determined by the resolution function. For the IEEE 1164 package, the resolution function is essentially a lookup table. Provided with the signal values from two drivers, the table returns the signal value to be assigned. For example, if one source is driving the signal to 1 and a second source's output is left floating (i.e., in state z), the resulting value will be 1. Alternatively, if the two sources are driving the shared signal to 1 and 0, respectively, the resulting value will be unknown, or x. The resolution function for the std_logic and std_logic_vector types is provided by the std_logic_1164 package. Having multiple drivers for a signal whose type is an unresolved type will result in an error. The user may define new resolved types and provide the resolution functions for their use.

We will leave resolution functions for the moment and return to them in greater detail when we deal with the creation and use of procedures and functions in Chapter 13. However, in the remainder of this text, all of the examples use the IEEE 1164 resolved single-bit and multibit types std_logic and std_logic_vector, respectively, rather than the unresolved types std_ulogic and std_ulogic_vector.

Simulation Exercise 10.1: A First Simulation Model

This exercise introduces the construction and simulation of simple VHDL models.

Step 1. Using a text editor, create a VHDL model of the full adder shown in Figure 10-3. Do not use a word processor, even though it may have an option for saving your text as an ASCII file. Some word processors place control characters in the file or may handle some characters nonuniformly (for example, left and right quotation marks). This can lead to analyzer errors. (However, you could correct such errors at the time that they are introduced.) Set the gate delays to 3 ns for the EX-OR gates and to 2 ns for all of the other gates.

Step 2. Use the types `std_logic` and `std_logic_vector` for the input and output signals. Declare and reference the library `IEEE` and the package `std_logic_1164`.

Step 3. Compile and load the model for simulation using a VHDL simulator toolset.

Step 4. Generate a waveform on each of the input signals.

Step 5. Run the simulation for 40 ns, and trace (i) the input signals; (ii) the internal signals `s1`, `s2`, and `s3`; and (iii) the `sum` and `carry` outputs.

Step 6. Check and list scheduled events on the internal signals and output signals.

Step 7. Pick an event on one of the input signals. Record the propagation of the effect of this event through the signal trace. Study the trace, and ensure that the model is operating correctly.

Step 8. Repeat this example, only this time do not initialize one of the input signals. What does the resulting trace look like, and what is the significance of the values on this uninitialized input?

End Simulation Exercise 10.1

Conditional Signal Assignment

The simple concurrent signal assignment statements that we have seen so far use Boolean expressions to compute the value of the target signal. The values of the signals on the RHS of the signal assignment statement are used to compute the value of the target signal. This new value is scheduled at some point in the future, using the **after** keyword. Expressing values of signals in this manner is convenient for describing combinational circuits whose behavior can be expressed with Boolean equations. However, we often need to model high-level circuits that require a richer set of constructs, such as multiplexors and decoders.

For example, consider the physical behavior of the 4-to-1 8-bit multiplexor described in Figure 10-5. The value of z is one of `In0`, `In1`, `In2`, or `In3`. The waveform that appears on one of the inputs is transferred to the output z. The specific choice depends upon the value of the control signals `S0` and `S1`, for which there are four possible alternatives. Each of these alternatives must be tested and one chosen.

```
library IEEE;
use IEEE.std_logic_1164.all;
entity mux4 is
port (In0, In1, In2, In3 : in std_logic_vector (7 downto 0);
        S0, S1: in std_logic;
            Z : out std_logic_vector (7 downto 0));
end mux4;

architecture behavioral of mux4 is
begin
Z <= In0 after 5 ns when S0 = '0' and S1 = '0' else
        In1 after 5 ns when S0 = '0' and S1 = '1' else
        In2 after 5 ns when S0 = '1' and S1 = '0' else
        In3 after 5 ns when S0 = '1' and S1 = '1' else
        "00000000" after 5 ns;
end behavioral;
```

FIGURE 10-5 Conditional signal assignment statement.

This behavior is captured in the conditional signal assignment statement. The structure of the statement follows from the physical behavior of the circuit. For each of the four possible values of S0 and S1, a waveform is specified. In this case, the waveform is composed of a single waveform element describing the most recent signal value on that input. As previously pointed out, more than one waveform element in each line of the conditional statement could have been specified, producing a waveform on the output signal Z.

In the corresponding physical circuit, an event on any one of the input signals, In0–In3, or any of the control signals, S0 or S1, may cause a change in the value of the output signal. Therefore, whenever any such event takes place, the concurrent signal assignment statement is executed and all four conditions may be checked. The order of the statements is important. The expressions on the RHS are evaluated in the order that they appear. The first conditional expression that is found to be true determines the value that is transferred to the output. Therefore, we must be careful to order the conditional expressions on the RHS to reflect the order in which they would be evaluated in the corresponding physical system. A careful look at the example in Figure 10-5 reveals that, in this case, only one expression can be true and therefore that the order does not matter in this particular example. Finally, note that even though there several lines of text in Figure 10-5, these lines correspond to only one signal assignment statement.

Selected Signal Assignment Statement

The selected signal assignment statement is very similar to the conditional signal assignment statement. The value of a signal is determined by the value of a *select expression*. For example, consider the operation of reading the value of a register from a register file with eight registers. Depending upon the value of the address, the contents of the appropriate register are selected. An example of a read-only register file with two read ports is shown in Figure 10-6.

This statement operates very much like a case statement in conventional programming languages. As a result, its semantics are somewhat distinct from those of conditional signal assignment statements. First, the choices are not evaluated in sequence. All choices are evaluated, but only one must be true. Furthermore, all of the choices that the programmer specifies must cover all of the possible choices. For example, consider the statement shown in Figure 10-6. Assume that we have only four registers, but both `addr1` and `addr2` are 3-bit addresses and therefore can address up to eight registers. The VHDL language requires you to specify the action to be taken if `addr1` or `addr2` takes on any of the eight values, including those between 4 and 7. This requirement is not really restrictive, since in practice we must consider what would happen in the physical system in such cases. The **others** keyword is used to state the value of the target signal over a range of values and thereby cover the whole range. Finally, the select expression can be quite flexible; for example, it can incorporate Boolean expressions.

As with simple and conditional CSAs, we must be aware of the conditions under which a selected signal assignment statement is executed. When an event occurs on a signal used in the select expression or any of the signals used in one of the choices, the statement is executed. This follows the expected behavior of the corresponding physical

```
library IEEE;
use IEEE.std_logic_1164.all;

entity reg_file is
port (addr1, addr2: in std_logic_vector (2 downto 0);
        reg_out_1, reg_out_2: out std_logic_vector (31 downto 0));
end reg_file;

architecture behavior of reg_file is
signal reg0, reg2, reg4, reg6: std_logic_vector (31 downto 0):=
        to_stdlogicvector(x"12345678");
signal reg1, reg3, reg5, reg7: std_logic_vector (31 downto 0):=
        to_stdlogicvector(x"abcdef00");
begin
with addr1 select
reg_out_1 <= reg0 after 5 ns when "000",
                        reg1 after 5 ns when "001",
                        reg2 after 5 ns when "010",
                        reg3 after 5 ns when "011",
                        reg3 after 5 ns when others;

with addr2 select
reg_out_2 <= reg0 after 5 ns when "000",
                        reg1 after 5 ns when "001",
                        reg2 after 5 ns when "010",
                        reg3 after 5 ns when "011",
                        reg3 after 5 ns when others;
end behavior;
```

FIGURE 10-6 Selected signal assignment statement.

implementation where an event on any of the addresses or register contents could potentially change the value of the output signal.

Note a few new statements in this example. First, we initialize the values of the registers when they are declared. In this example, the even-numbered registers are initialized with a hexadecimal value denoted by x"12345678", while the odd-numbered registers are initialized with the hexadecimal value denoted by x"abcdef00". Note that the target is a signal of type std_logic_vector. The hexadecimal values must be converted to the type std_logic_vector before they can be assigned. On the other hand, if the values were specified in binary notation, explicit type conversion would not be required. The function to_stdlogicvector () is in the package std_logic_1164 and performs this type of conversion operation. To promote portability in this text, we retain explicit type conversion where necessary in all of the examples. Type conversion as well as other functions in support of the IEEE 1164 value system are found in the std_logic_1164 package provided by practically all CAD tool vendors. There are also other packages of functions and procedures that are provided by the vendors. Many standardization efforts are underway within the community in an effort to ensure portability of models between vendor toolsets and cooperating designers. These packages also provide similar type conversion functions, often with slightly different names. Check the availability of such packages within your toolset, and browse through them. The packages may be located in the IEEE library, but be aware that in some systems, they may be located in another design library. In the latter case, a new **library** clause is required to declare this library, and the **use** clause must be appropriately modified to reference this library rather than IEEE. The use of libraries and packages is presented in greater detail in Chapter 13.

Constructing VHDL Models Using CSAs

Armed with concurrent signal assignment statements, we are now ready to construct VHDL models of interesting classes of digital systems. This section provides a prescription for constructing such VHDL models. By following this mechanical approach to constructing models, we can generate an intuition about the structure of VHDL programs and the utility of the language constructs discussed so far.

In a VHDL model written using only concurrent signal assignment statements, the execution of a signal assignment statement is initiated by the flow of data or signal values rather than the textual order of the statements. Based on the language features we have seen thus far, a model of a digital system will be composed of an entity–architecture pair. The architecture model, in turn, will be composed of some combination of simple, conditional, and selected signal assignment statements. The architecture may also declare and use internal signals in addition to the input and output ports declared in the entity description.

The following description assumes that we are writing a VHDL model of a gate-level combinational circuit. However, the approach can certainly be applied to higher level systems by using combinational building blocks such as encoders and multiplexors. The simple methodology comprises two steps: (i) the drawing of an annotated schematic and (ii) the conversion to a VHDL description. The following procedure outlines a few simple steps to organize the information we have about the physical system prior to writing the VHDL model:

Construct_Schematic

1. Represent each component (e.g., gate) of the system to be modeled as a *delay element*. The delay element simply captures all of the delays associated with the computation represented by the component and propagation of signals through the component. For each output signal of a component, associate a specific value of delay through the component.

2. Draw a schematic interconnecting all of the delay elements. Uniquely label each component.

3. Identify the input signals of the circuit as input ports.

4. Identify the output signals of the circuit as output ports.

5. All remaining signals are internal signals.

6. Associate a type with each input, output, and internal signal, such as `std_logic` or `std_logic_vector`.

7. Ensure that each input port, output port, and internal signal is labeled with a unique name.

An example of such a schematic is shown in Figure 10-7. Now, from this schematic, we can use concurrent signal assignment statements to write a VHDL model. A template for the VHDL description is shown in Figure 10-8. This template can be filled in as described in the next procedure, **Construct_CSA_Model.**

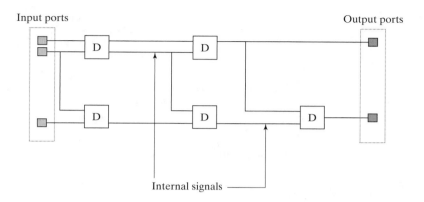

FIGURE 10-7 Delay-element model of a digital system.

Construct_CSA_Model

1. At this point, it is recommended that the IEEE 1164 value system be used. To do so, include the following two lines at the top of your model's declaration:

   library IEEE;
   use IEEE.std_logic_1164.all;

   Single-bit signals can be declared to be of type std_logic, while multibit quantities can be declared to be of type std_logic_vector.

2. Select a name for the entity (entity_name) and write the entity description, specifying each input or output signal port, its mode, and its associated type. This type can be read off of the annotated schematic.

3. Select a name for the architecture (arch_name) and write the architecture description. Place both the entity and architecture descriptions in the same file.

   3.1 Within the architecture description, name and declare all of the internal signals used to connect the components. The declaration states the type of each signal and its initial value. Initialization is not required, but is recommended. These declarations occur prior to the first **begin** statement in the architecture.

```
library library-name-1,  library-name-2;
use library-name-1.package-name.all;
use library-name-2.package-name.all;
entity entity_name is
port ( input signals  :  in type;
        output signals :  out type) ;
end entity_name;

architecture arch_name of entity_name is

-- declare internal signals
-- you may have multiple signals of different types
signal internal-signal-1 : type := initialization;
signal internal-signal-2 : type := initialization;

begin

-- specify value of each signal as a function of
other signals
internal-signal-1 <= simple, conditional, or selected CSA;
internal-signal-2 <= simple, conditional, or selected CSA;
output-signal-1   <= simple, conditional, or selected CSA;
output-signal-2   <= simple, conditional, or selected CSA;

end arch_name;
```

FIGURE 10-8 A template for using CSAs to write VHDL models.

3.2   Each internal signal should be driven by exactly one component. If this is not the case, make sure that the type of the signal is a resolved type, such as `std_logic` or `std_logic_vector`. For each internal signal, write a concurrent signal assignment statement that expresses the value of this internal signal as a function of the component input signals that are used to compute its value. Use the delay value associated with that output signal for that component.

3.3   Each output port signal is driven by the output of some internal component. For each output port signal, write a concurrent signal assignment statement that expresses its value as some function of the signals that are inputs to that component.

3.4 If you are using any functions or type definitions provided by a third party, make sure that you have declared the appropriate library, using the **library** clause, and declared the use of this package via the presence of a **use** clause in your model.

If there are *S* signals and ports in the schematic, there will be *S* concurrent signal assignment statements in the VHDL model—one for each signal. This approach provides a quick way of constructing VHDL models by attempting to maintain a close correspondence with the hardware being modeled. There are many alternatives to constructing a VHDL model, and the above approach represents only one method. With experience, the reader will no doubt discover many other ways to construct efficient models for digital systems of interest.

Simulation Exercise 10.2: A 1-Bit ALU

Consider the simple 1-bit ALU shown in Figure 10-9, which performs the AND, OR, and addition operations. The result produced at the ALU output depends on the value of signal OPCODE. Write and simulate a model of this ALU, using concurrent signal assignment statements. Test each OPCODE to ensure that the model is accurate by examining the waveforms on the input and output signals. Use a gate delay of 5 ns and a delay of 2 ns through the multiplexor. Remember, while the OPCODE field is 2 bits wide, there are only three valid inputs to the multiplexor.

Step 1. Follow the steps in **Construct_Schematic**. Ensure that all of the signals, including the input and output ports, are defined and labeled and their mode and types are specified.

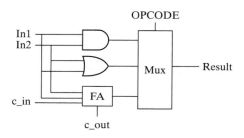

FIGURE 10-9 A single-bit ALU (FA = full adder).

Step 2. Follow the steps in **Construct_CSA_Model**. To describe the operation of the full adder, use two simple concurrent signal assignment statements: one each to describe the computation of the `sum` and `carry` outputs, respectively. Call this file alu.vhd.

Step 3. Compile alu.vhd.

Step 4. Load the simulation model into the simulator.

Step 5. Generate a sequence of inputs that you can use to verify that the model is functioning correctly.

Step 6. Open a trace window with the signals you would like to trace. Include internal signals, which are signals that are not entity ports in the model.

Step 7. Run the simulation for 50 ns.

Step 8. Check the trace to determine correctness.

Step 9. Print and record the trace.

Step 10. Add new operations to the single-bit ALU; then recompile and resimulate the model. For example, you can add the exclusive-OR, subtraction, and complement operations.

End Simulation Exercise 10.2

Delta Delays

What happens if we do not specify a delay for the occurrence of an event on a signal? For example, the computation of the outputs for an exclusive-OR gate may be written as follows:

```
sum <= (a xor b);
```

We may choose to ignore delays when we do not know what they are or when we are interested only in creating a simulation that is functionally correct and is not concerned with the timing behavior. For example, consider the timing of the full-adder model shown in Figure 10-4. There is a correct ordering of events on the signals. Input events on signals `In1`, `In2`, and `c_in` produce events on internal signals `s1`, `s2`, and `s3`, which, in turn, produce events on the output signals `sum` and `c_out`. For functional correctness, we must maintain this ordering even when delays remain unspecified. This effect is achieved within the VHDL language by defining an infinitesimally small delay referred to as a *delta delay*. This form of the signal assignment statement implicitly places an **after** 0 **ns** time expression following the value expression.

When this syntax is used, component is effectively assigned a delay value of Δ. Now simulation proceeds exactly as described in the earlier examples. As the next example will demonstrate, Δ does not actually have to be assigned a value, but is used within the simulator to order events. If events with zero delay are produced at timestep T, the simulator simply organizes and processes events in time order of occurrence: Events that occur Δ seconds later are followed by events occurring 2Δ seconds later, followed by events occurring 3Δ seconds later, and so on. Delta delays are simply used to enforce dependencies between events and thereby ensure correct simulation. The following example will help clarify the use of delta delays.

Example: Delta Delays

Consider the combinational logic circuit and the corresponding VHDL code shown in Figure 10-10. The model captures a behavioral description of the circuit without specifying any gate delays.

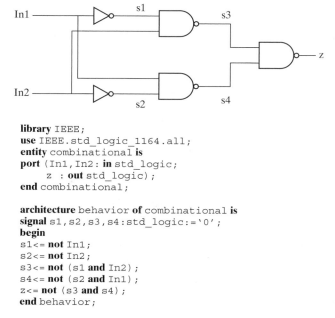

```vhdl
library IEEE;
use IEEE.std_logic_1164.all;
entity combinational is
port (In1,In2: in std_logic;
      z  : out std_logic);
end combinational;

architecture behavior of combinational is
signal s1,s2,s3,s4:std_logic:='0';
begin
s1<= not In1;
s2<= not In2;
s3<= not (s1 and In2);
s4<= not (s2 and In1);
z<= not (s3 and s4);
end behavior;
```

FIGURE 10-10 A VHDL model with delta delays.

Figure 10-11(a) illustrates the timing of the circuit when inputs are applied as shown. At time 10 ns, the signal In2 makes a $1 \rightarrow 0$ transition. This transition causes a sequence of events in the circuit to

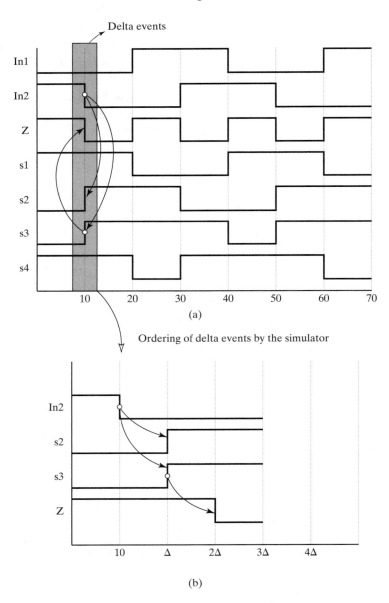

(a)

(b)

FIGURE 10-11 (a) Occurrence of delta events. (b) Ordering imposed on these events within the simulator.

occur, resulting in the value of z = 0. From the accompanying VHDL code, we see that the gate delays are implicitly 0 ns. Therefore, the timing diagram shows the signal z acquiring this value at the same instant in time that In2 makes a transition. From the timing diagram, it is also clear that signals s2 and s3 make transitions at this instant in time as well. In reality, we know from the circuit diagram that there is a dependency between In2 and s3, and s3 and z. These dependencies are evident from the structure of the circuit. The event on In2 precedes and causes the transitions on s3 and s4, while the transition on s3 causes the transition on z. The simulation of the circuit honors these dependencies through the logical use of delta delays. The dependencies between In2, s3, and z are shown in Figure 10-11(b). The transition on In2 causes s3 to make a transition to 1 after Δ seconds. The event on s3 causes a $1 \rightarrow 0$ event on z after 2Δ seconds. These events are referred to as delta events and are shown in Figure 10-11(b). These delta events take place within the simulator and do not appear on the external trace produced for the viewer (i.e., Figure 10-11(a)). The actual implementation of delta events is managed within the simulator by keeping track of signal values and the times at which they are updated.

By forcing all events to take some infinitesimally small amount of time, the dependencies between events can be preserved and the correct operation of the circuit maintained. Recall how the circuit is simulated: Time is advanced to that of the first event on the list. The signal is assigned this value, any new outputs are computed, and the process is repeated. When time is advanced by Δ, this step is referred to as a delta cycle.

Example End: Delta Delays

Simulation Exercise 10.3: Delta Delays

Repeat the simulation of the full-adder model in Simulation Exercise 10.1, but do not specify any gate delays.

Step 1. Run the simulation for 40 ns, and trace input, internal, and output signals.

Step 2. Annotate the trace to identify delta events.

Step 3. Compare the trace generated here with that generated in Simulation Exercise 10.1. What are the differences?

Step 4. Modify the model to include a 2-ns wire delay for internal signals. Recompile the model.

Step 5. Simulate the new model, and generate another trace. The effect of wire delays is now explicitly captured.

Step 6. Identify events that occur in this second trace that are different from those in the earlier trace.

Step 7. Create an input stimulus for one of the inputs with pulses whose duration are both shorter and longer than the gate delay. Set the value of the remaining inputs to logic 0. This is usually achieved by adjusting the simulator step time and via stimulus commands unique to the simulator that you are using.

Step 8. Generate a trace, and identify pulses that are rejected by the gate models.

End Simulation Exercise 10.3

Chapter Summary

The reader should be comfortable with the following concepts that have been introduced in this chapter:

- Entity and architecture constructs
- Concurrent signal assignment statements
  - ◆ simple concurrent signal assignment
  - ◆ conditional concurrent signal assignment
  - ◆ selected concurrent signal assignment
- Using concurrent signal assignment statements to construct models
  - ◆ modeling events, propagation delays, and concurrency
- Modeling delays
  - ◆ delta delay
- Signal drivers and projected waveforms
- Shared signals, resolved types, and resolution functions

- Using waveform elements to generate waveforms
- Events and transactions

A syntactic reference to common language types and operators can be found in the VHDL reference manual provided in electronic form with the software.

The VHDL models of systems should now be beginning to take some form. The reader should be capable of constructing functionally correct models for many types of digital systems.

Exercises

1. A good exercise for understanding entity descriptions is to write the entity descriptions for components found in data books from component vendors—for example, the TTL data book. These entity descriptions can be compiled without the architecture descriptions and thus can be checked for syntactic correctness. Of course, we cannot say anything about the semantic correctness of such descriptions, since we have not even written the architecture descriptions yet!

2. Write and simulate a VHDL model of a 2-bit comparator.

3. Sketch the output waveform produced by the following VHDL simple concurrent signal assignment statements:

    s1 <= '0' **after** 5 **ns**, '1' **after** 15 **ns**, '0' **after** 35 **ns**, '1' **after** 50 **ns**;

    s1 <= '0' **after** 20 **ns**, '1' **after** 25 **ns**, '0' **after** 50 **ns**;

4. Construct and test VHDL modules for generating the periodic waveforms with the structure shown in Figure 10-12.

5. Construct a VHDL model that will accept a clock signal as input and produce the complement signal as output with a delay of 10 ns.

6. Write and simulate the entity–architecture description of a 3-bit decoder, using the conditional signal assignment statement. Test the model with all possible combinations of inputs, and plot the decoder's output waveform.

7. Repeat the preceding exercise by building the decoder from basic gates. Is there any difference between the number of

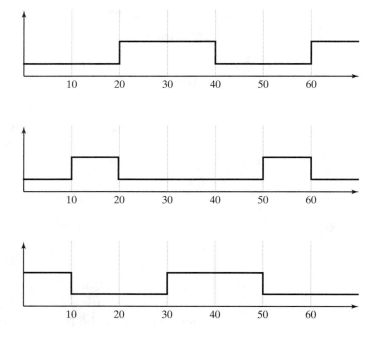

FIGURE 10-12 Sample waveforms.

events generated in the simulation of this model and in a model where the behavior is described using the conditional signal assignment statement? You should be able to answer this question by examining the traces in both cases over the same time interval. If your simulator permits, examine the event queues during simulation.

8.   Why are the concepts of delta events and delta delays necessary for the correct discrete-event simulation of digital circuits?

11

Modeling Behavior

This chapter expands upon the approach described so far that uses concurrent signal assignment statements for constructing VHDL models. In Chapter 10, components were modeled as delay elements, and their internal behavior was described using concurrent signal assignment statements. In this chapter, we discuss more powerful constructs for describing the internal behavior of components when they cannot be simply modeled as delay elements. The basis for these descriptions is the *process* construct, which enables us to use conventional programming language constructs and idioms. As a result, we can model the behavior of components much more complex than delay elements and are able to model systems at higher levels of abstraction.

The Process Construct

The VHDL language and modeling concepts described in the previous chapter were derived from the operational characteristics of digital circuits, where the design is represented as a schematic of concurrently operating components. Each component is characterized by the generation of events on output signals in response to events on input signals. These output events may occur after a component-dependent propagation delay. The component behavior is expressed using a CSA (Concurrent Signal Assignment) statement, that explicitly relates input signals, output signals, and propagation delays. Such models are convenient to construct when components correspond to gates or switch-level models of transistors. However, when we wish to construct models of complex components such as CPUs, memory modules, or communication protocols, such a model of behavior can be quite limiting. The event model is still valid; externally, we see that events on the input signals will eventually cause events on the output signals of the component. However, the computation of the time at which these output events will occur and the value of the output signals can be quite complex. Moreover, for modeling components such as memories, we need to retain state information within the component description. It is not sufficient to be able to compute the values of the output signals as a function of the values of the input signals.

Modeling a Memory Module

For example, consider the behavior of a simple model of a memory module as shown in Figure 11-1. The memory module is provided with address, data, read, and write control signals. Let us assume that it contains 4,096 32-bit words of memory. The values of the R and W control signals determine whether the data on DI are to be written at the address on the ADDR port or whether data are to be read from that address and provided on the output port DO. The signal S is used to indicate completion of the memory operation. Events on the input address, data, or control lines produce events that cause the memory model to be executed. We can also reasonably expect to know the memory access times for read and write operations and therefore know the propagation delays. However, the behavior internal to the memory module is difficult to describe using only the signal assignment statements provided in Chapter 10. How can we represent memory words? How can we address the correct word, based on the values of the address lines and control signals? The answers are easier to come by if we have access to conventional sequential programming-language constructs. Memory can be implemented as an array, and the

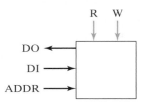

FIGURE 11-1 A model of memory.

address value can be used to index this array. Depending upon the value of the control signals, we can decide whether this array element is to be written or read. Such behavior can be realized in VHDL by using *sequential statements* via the *process* construct.

In contrast to concurrent signal assignment statements, a process is a sequentially executed block of code. A VHDL model of a memory module equivalent to the one in Figure 11-1 is shown in Figure 11-2. This model consists of one process that is labeled `mem_process`. Process labels are delimited by colons. The structure of a process is very similar to that of programs written in a conventional block-structured programming language such as C++. The process begins with a declarative region followed by the process body, which is delimited by **begin** and **end** keywords. Variables and constants used within the process are declared within the declarative region. The **begin** keyword denotes the start of the computational part of the process. All of the statements in the process are executed sequentially. Data structures may include arrays and queues, and programs may use standard data types such as integers, characters, and real numbers. Unlike signals, whose changes in values must be scheduled to occur at discrete points in time, variable assignments take effect immediately. Variable assignment is denoted by the := operator. Since all statements are executed sequentially within a process, values assigned to variables are visible to all following statements within that same process. Control flow within a process is strictly sequentially altered by constructs such as **if–then–else** or **loop** statements. In fact, we can regard the process itself as a traditional sequential program.

One of the distinguishing features of processes is that we can make assignments to signals declared external to the process. For example, consider the memory model in Figure 11-2. At the end of this process, we have signal assignment statements that assign internally computed values to signals in the interface after a specified propagation delay. Thus, externally, we are able to maintain the discrete-event execution model: Events on the memory inputs produce events on the memory outputs after a delay equal to the memory access time. However, internally, we are able to develop complex models of behavior that produce these external events. *With respect to simulation time, a process executes in zero time.* Delays are associated only with the assignment of values to signals.

```vhdl
library IEEE;
use IEEE.std_logic_1164.all;
use WORK.std_logic_arith.all;
        -- we need this package for 1164-related functions
entity memory is
port(address, write_data : in std_logic_vector (31 downto 0);
        MemWrite, MemRead : in std_logic;
        read_data : out std_logic_vector (31 downto 0));
end memory;

architecture behavioral of memory is
type mem_array is array(0 to 7) of std_logic_vector (31 downto 0);

begin

mem_process: process (address, write_data)

variable data_mem : mem_array := (
        to_stdlogicvector(X"00000000"), --- initialize memory
        to_stdlogicvector(X"00000000"),
        to_stdlogicvector(X"00000000"),
        to_stdlogicvector(X"00000000"),
        to_stdlogicvector(X"00000000"),
        to_stdlogicvector(X"00000000"),
        to_stdlogicvector(X"00000000"),
        to_stdlogicvector(X"00000000"));
variable addr : integer;

begin

        -- the following type conversion function is in std_logic_arith

        addr := to_integer (address (2 downto 0));
        if MemWrite = '1' then
        data_mem(addr) := write_data;

        elsif MemRead = '1' then
        read_data <= data_mem(addr) after 10 ns;
        end if;
end process mem_process;

end behavioral;
```

FIGURE 11-2 A behavioral description of a memory module.

Recall that a CSA is executed anytime an event occurs on a signal on the right-hand side of the signal assignment statement. When is a process executed? In Figure 11-2, adjacent to the **process** keyword is a list of input signals to the component. This list is referred to as the *sensitivity list*. The execution of a process is initiated whenever an event occurs on any of the signals in the sensitivity list of the process. Once started, the process executes to completion in zero (simulation) time and potentially generates a new set of events on output signals. We now begin to see the similarity between a process and a CSA. In the models with concurrent signal assignment statements, input signals are inferred by their presence on the right-hand side of the signal assignment statement. In a process, the signals can be listed in the sensitivity list. For all practical purposes, we can regard a process simply as a big concurrent signal assignment statement that executes simultaneously with other processes and signal assignment statements. Processes are simply capable of describing more complex events than the CSAs described in Chapter 10. *In fact, CSAs are themselves processes!* However, they are special cases and do not require the **process**, **begin**, and **end** syntax of more complex processes.

You will notice the use of another package in the model shown in Figure 11-2: `std_logic_arith`. The definition of the type conversion function `to_integer()` is in this package. This function is necessary because memory is modeled as an array of 32-bit words. This array is indexed by an integer. Therefore, the memory address, which is provided as a 32-bit number of type `std_logic_vector`, must be converted to an integer before this array can be accessed. Of course we do not create an array with 2^{32} entries, but rather eight words of memory. Therefore, the model uses only the lower 3 bits of the memory address. In this model and a few others in this text, we have used the package `std_logic_arith`. We have compiled this model into the library WORK. This library is the default working directory and is implicitly declared. We do not need a **library** clause in our model. Many vendors will support a number of packages with many useful type conversion, arithmetic, and logic functions. These packages will be placed in various libraries. Check with your installation to determine the location and contents of available packages. This is all we need to know on this topic for the moment. We will revisit packages and libraries in greater detail in Chapter 13, "Subprograms, Packages, and Libraries."

Since statements within a process are executed sequentially, these statements are referred to as *sequential statements*, in contrast to the concurrent signal assignment statements that we saw in Chapter 10. Processes can be thought of as programs that are executed within the simulation in order to model the behavior of a component. Thus, we have more powerful means to model the behavior of digital systems. Such models are often referred to as behavioral models, although any VHDL model using concurrent or sequential statements is a description of behavior.

Once the concepts of a process and the underlying semantics are understood, we need to know the syntax of the major programming constructs that we can use within a process. Identifiers, operators, and useful data types are provided in Chapter 14, "Identifiers, Data Types, and Operators." Based on our experience with other high level-languages, we can immediately begin to describe the behavior of components and to develop nontrivial simulation models.

Programming Constructs

if–then–else

An **if** statement is executed by evaluating an expression and conditionally executing a block of sequential statements. The structure may optionally include an **else** component. The statement may also include zero or more **elsif** branches. (Note the absence of the letter "e" in **elsif**.) In this case, all of the Boolean-valued expressions are evaluated sequentially until the first true expression is encountered. An **if** statement is closed by the **end if** clause. A good example of the utility of the **if–then–else** construct is captured in the memory model of Figure 11-2.

Concurrent Processes and the case Statement

The behavioral model shown in Figure 11-2 uses a single process. Just as we had concurrent signal assignment statements, we may also have concurrently executing processes. Consider another behavioral model of a half-adder with two processes as shown in Figure 11-3.

```vhdl
library IEEE;
use IEEE.std_logic_1164.all;

entity half_adder is
port (a, b : in std_logic;
      sum, carry : out std_logic);
end half_adder;

architecture behavior of half_adder is
begin

sum_proc: process(a,b)
begin
      if (a = b) then
            sum <= '0' after 5 ns;
      else
            sum <= (a or b) after 5 ns;
      end if;
end process;


carry_proc: process (a,b)
begin
      case a is
      when '0' =>
            carry <= a after 5 ns;
      when '1' =>
            carry <= b after 5 ns;
      when others =>
            carry <= 'X' after 5 ns;
      end case;
end process carry_proc;


end behavior;
```

FIGURE 11-3 A two-process half-adder model.

Both processes are sensitive to events on the input signals a and b. Whenever an event occurs on either a or b, both processes are activated and execute concurrently in simulation time. The second process is structured using a **case** statement. The **case** statement is used whenever it is necessary to select one of several branches of execution, based on the value of an expression. The branches of the **case** statement must cover all possible values of the expression being tested. Each value of the case expression being tested can belong to only one branch of the **case** statement. The **others** clause can be used to ensure that all possible values for the **case** expression are covered. Although this example shows a single statement within each branch, in general the branch can be composed of a sequence of sequential statements. This example also shows that port signals are visible within a process. This means that process statements can read port values and schedule values on output ports.

Loops

There are two forms of loop statements. The first form is **for** loops. An example of the use of such a loop construct is shown in Figure 11-4. This example multiplies two 32-bit numbers by successively shifting the multiplicand and adding to the partial product if the corresponding bit of the multiplier is 1. The model simply implements what we have traditionally known as long multiplication, using base-2 arithmetic. The model saves storage by using the lower half of the 64-bit product register to initially store the multiplier. As successive bits of the multiplier are examined, the bits in the lower half of the product register are shifted out, eventually leaving a 64-bit product. Note the use of the **&** operator, representing concatenation. A logical shift-right operation is specified by copying the upper 63 (out of 64) bits into the lower 63 bits of the product register and setting the most significant bit to 0, using the concatenation operator.

There are several unique features of this form of a loop statement. Note that the loop index is not declared anywhere within the process! The loop index is automatically and implicitly declared by virtue of its use within the loop statement. Moreover, the loop index is declared locally for this loop. So if a variable or signal with the name `index` is used elsewhere within the same process or architecture (but not in the same loop), it is treated as a distinct object. Unlike in other languages, the loop index cannot be assigned a value or altered in the body of the loop. Therefore, loop indices cannot be provided as parameters via a procedure call or as an input port. We see that the loop index is exactly that—a loop index—and the language prevents us from using it in any other fashion. This factor does make it convenient to write loops, since we do not have to worry about our choice of variable names for the loop index conflicting with variable names elsewhere in the model.

Often, it is necessary to continue the iteration until some condition is satisfied rather than performing a fixed number of iterations. The second form of the loop statement is the **while** construct. In this form, the **for** statement is simply replaced by

> **while** (*condition*) **loop**

Unlike the **for** construct, the condition may involve variables that are modified within the loop. For example, the **for** loop in Figure 11-4 could be replaced by the following:

```
while  j < 32  loop
   . . .
   . . .
   j := j+1;
end  loop;
```

More on Processes

Upon initialization, all processes are executed once. Thereafter, processes are executed in a data-driven manner: activated by events on signals in the sensitivity list of the process or by waiting for the occurrence of specific events via the **wait** statement (described on page 148). Remember that the sensitivity list of a process is not a parameter list! This list simply identifies those signals to which the process is sensitive. When an event occurs on any one of these signals, the process is executed. This construct is analogous to CSAs, which are executed whenever an event occurs on a signal on the right-hand side of the CSA. In fact, CSAs are really processes with simpler syntax. All of the ports of the entity and the signals declared within an architecture are visible within a process, which means that they can be read or assigned values from within a process. Thus, during the course of execution, a process may read or write any of the

```
library IEEE;
use IEEE.std_logic_1164.all;
use WORK.std_logic_arith.all; -- needed for arithmetic functions

entity mult32 is
port (multiplicand, multiplier : in std_logic_vector(31 downto 0);
        product : out std_logic_vector (63 downto 0));
end mult32;

architecture behavioral of mult32 is
constant module_delay: Time:= 10 ns;
begin

mult_process: process(multiplicand,multiplier)
variable product_register : std_logic_vector (63 downto 0) :=
        to_stdlogicvector(X"0000000000000000");
variable multiplicand_register : std_logic_vector(31 downto 0):=
        to_stdlogicvector(X"00000000");

begin
multiplicand_register := multiplicand;
product_register(63 downto 0) :=
to_stdlogicvector(X"00000000") & multiplier;
--
-- repeated shift-and-add loop
--
for index in 1 to 32 loop
        if product_register(0) = '1' then
                product_register(63 downto 32) :=
                        product_register(63 downto 32)
                        + multiplicand_register(31 downto 0);
        end if;
        -- perform a right shift with zero fill
        product_register (63 downto 0) :=
                '0' & product_register (63 downto 1);
end loop;

-- write result to output port
product <= product_register after module_delay;

end process mult_process;

end behavioral;
```

FIGURE 11-4 An example of the use of the loop construct.

signals declared in the architecture or any of the ports on the entity. This is how processes can communicate among themselves, for example. Process *A* may write a signal that is in the sensitivity list of Process *B*. This will cause Process *B* to execute. Process *B* may in turn similarly write a signal in the sensitivity list of Process *A*. The use of communicating processes is elaborated in the following example.

Example: Communicating Processes

This example illustrates a model of a full adder constructed from two half-adders and a two-input OR gate, shown in Figure 11-5. The behaviors of the three components are described using processes that communicate through signals. When there is an event on either input signal, process HA1 executes, creating events on internal signals s1 and s2. These signals are in the sensitivity lists of processes HA2 and O1, and therefore these processes will execute and schedule events on their outputs as necessary. Note that this style of modeling still follows the structural description of the hardware, where we have one process for each hardware component of the figure. Contrast this model with the model described in Figure 10-3.

Example End: Communicating Processes

Simulation Exercise 11.1: Combinational Shift Logic

This exercise is concerned with the construction of the combinational-logic shifter shown in Figure 11-6. The inputs to the shift logic include a 3-bit operand specifying the shift amount, two single-bit signals identifying the direction of the shift operation—left or right—and an 8-bit operand. The output of the shift logic is the shifted 8-bit operand. Shift operations provide zero fill. For example, a left shift of the number 01101111 by three bit positions will produce the output 01111000.

Step 1.   Create a text file with the entity description and the architecture description of the shift logic. Assume that the delay through the shift logic is fixed at 40 ns, independent of the number of digits that are shifted. While you can implement this behavior in many ways, for this assignment use a single process and the sequential VHDL statements to implement the behavior of the shift logic. You might find it

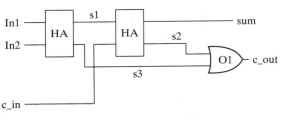

```
library IEEE;
use IEEE.std_logic_1164.all;

entity full_adder is
port (In1, c_in, In2 : in std_logic;
      sum, c_out : out std_logic);
end full_adder;

architecture behavioral of full_adder is
signal s1, s2, s3: std_logic;
constant delay :Time:= 5 ns;
begin

--process describing the first half-adder
HA1: process (In1, In2)
begin
        s1 <= (In1 xor In2) after delay;
        s3 <= (In1 and In2) after delay;
end process HA1;

--process describing the second half-adder
HA2: process (s1, c_in)
begin
        sum <= (s1 xor c_in) after delay;
        s2 <= (s1 and c_in) after delay;
end process HA2;

--process describing the two-input OR gate
OR1: process (s2, s3)
begin
        c_out <= (s2 or s3) after delay;
end process OR1;

end behavioral;
```

FIGURE 11-5 A communicating-process model of a full adder.

useful to use the concatenation operator, **&**, and addressing within arrays to perform the shift operations. For example, we can perform the following assignment:

dataout <= datain(4 **downto** 0) & "000";

This assignment statement will perform a left shift by three digits with zero fill. Both input and output operands are 8-bit numbers. For VHDL'93, you may use the VHDL built-in shift operators. Use the **case** statement to structure your process.

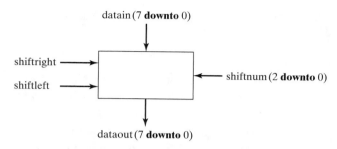

FIGURE 11-6 Interface description for a combinational-logic shifter.

Step 2. Use the types `std_logic` and `std_logic_vector` for the input and output signals. Declare and reference the library `IEEE` and the package `std_logic_1164`.

Step 3. Create a sequence of test vectors. Each of the test vectors will specify the values of (1) the `shiftright` and `shiftleft` single-bit control signals, (2) an 8-bit input operand, and (3) a 3-bit number that specifies the number of digits by which the input operand is to be shifted. Your test cases should be sufficient to ensure that the model is operating correctly.

Step 4. Load the simulation model into the simulator. Set the simulator step time to be equal to the value of the propagation delay through the shift logic.

Step 5. Using the facilities available within the simulator, generate the input stimulus and open a trace window to view both the input stimulus and the output operand value.

Step 6. Exercise the simulator by running the simulation long enough to cover your test cases. Verify correct operation from the trace.

Step 7. Once you have the simulation functioning correctly, modify your model to implement circular shift operations. These operations execute such that the digits that are shifted out of one end of the operand are the inputs to the other end. For example, a circular left shift of the pattern 10010111 by 3 digits will be 10111100. The circular shift operations can be implemented using the concatenation operator. In VHDL'93, the circular shift operations can be implemented with the VHDL predefined operators.

End Simulation Exercise 11.1

The wait Statement

The execution behavior of the models presented in Chapter 10 and the behavioral models described so far in this chapter have been data driven, where events on the input signals initiated the execution of processes. The processes would then suspend until the next event on a signal defined in its sensitivity list. This behavior fits well with the behavior of combinational circuits, where a change on the input signals may cause a change in the value of the output signals. Therefore the outputs should be recomputed whenever there is a change in the value of the input signal.

However, what about modeling circuits for which the outputs are computed only at specific points in time independently of events on the inputs? And how do we model circuits that respond only to certain events on the input signals? For example, in synchronous sequential circuits, the clock signal determines when the outputs may change or when inputs are read. Such behavior requires us to be able to specify in a more general manner the conditions under which the circuit outputs must be recomputed. In VHDL terms, we need a more general way of specifying when a process is executed or suspended pending the occurrence of an event or events. This capability is provided by the **wait** statement.

The various **wait** statements explicitly specify the conditions under which a process may resume execution after being suspended. The forms of the **wait** statement include the following:

> **wait for** *time expression*;
>
> **wait on** *signal*;
>
> **wait until** *condition*;
>
> **wait**;

The first form of the **wait** statement causes suspension of the process for a period of time given by the evaluation of *time expression*. This is an expression that should evaluate to a value that is of type **time**. An example of the simplest form of this statement is as follows:

> **wait for** 20 **ns**;

The second form causes a process to suspend execution until an event occurs on one or more signals in a group of signals. For example, we might have the following statement:

wait on `clk,reset,status`;

In this case, an event on any of the signals causes the process to resume execution with the first statement following the **wait** statement. The third form can specify a condition that evaluates to a Boolean value, TRUE or FALSE.

By using these **wait** statements, processes can be used to model components that are not necessarily data driven, but are driven only by certain types of events, such as the rising edge of a clock signal. Many such conditions cannot be described using sensitivity lists alone. More importantly, we would often like to construct models in which we need to suspend a process at multiple points within the process and not just at the beginning. Such models are made possible through the use of the **wait** statement. The following examples will help further motivate the use of the **wait** statement.

Example: Positive-Edge-Triggered D Flip-Flop

The model of a positive-edge-triggered D flip-flop is a good example of the use of the **wait** statement. The behavior of this component is such that the D input is sampled on the rising edge of the clock and transferred to the output. Therefore, the description of the model must be able to specify computations of output values only at specific points of time—in this case, the rising edge of the clock signal. This is done using the **wait** statement, as shown in Figure 11-7. This brings us to another very interesting feature of the language. Note the statement Clk'**event** in the model shown in Figure 11-7. This statement is true if an event (i.e., signal transition) has occurred on the Clk signal. The conjunction (Clk'**event and** Clk = '1'), is true for a rising edge on the Clk signal. The signal clock is said to have an *attribute* named **event** associated with it. The predicate Clk'**event** is true whenever an event has occurred on the signal Clk in the most recent simulation cycle. Recall that an event is a change in the signal value. In contrast, a *transaction* occurs on a signal when a new assignment has been made to the signal, but the value may not have changed. As this example illustrates, such an attribute is very useful. The next section lists some useful attributes of VHDL objects.

```
library IEEE;
use IEEE.std_logic_1164.all;
entity dff is
port (D, Clk : in std_logic;
      Q, Qbar : out std_logic);
end dff;

architecture behavioral of dff is
begin

output: process
begin
      wait until (Clk'event and Clk = '1');

      Q <= D after 5 ns;
      Qbar <= not D after 5 ns;
end process output;

end behavioral;
```

FIGURE 11-7 Behavioral model of a positive-edge-triggered D flip-flop.

The std_logic_1164 package also provides two useful functions that we could have used in lieu of attributes: rising_edge (Clk) and falling_edge (Clk). These functions take a signal of type std_logic as an argument and return a Boolean value denoting whether a rising edge or falling edge occurred on the signal, respectively. The predicate Clk'**event** simply denotes a change in value. Note that a single-bit signal of type std_logic can have up to nine values. Thus, if we are really looking for a rising edge from signal value 0 to 1, or a falling edge from signal value 1 to 0, it would be better to replace the test **if** (Clk'**event and** Clk = '1') with **if** rising_edge(Clk).

Continuing with the description of the operation of the D flip-flop, we see that the input is sampled on the rising clock edge, and the output values are scheduled after a period equal to the propagation delay through the flip-flop. The process is not executed whenever there is a change in the value of the input signal D, but rather only when there is a rising edge on the signal Clk.

Example End: Positive-Edge-Triggered D Flip-Flop

The preceding example did not specify the initial values of the flip-flop. When a physical system is powered up, the individual flip-flops may be initialized to some known state, but not necessarily all in the same state. In general, it is better to have some control over initial states of the flip-flops. This is usually achieved by providing such inputs as `Clear` or `Set` and `Preset` or `Reset`. Asserting the `Set` input forces Q to be 1, and asserting the `Reset` input forces Q to be 0. These signals override the effect of the clock signal and are active at any time, hence the characterization as asynchronous inputs, as opposed to the synchronous nature of the clock signal. The following example illustrates how we can extend the previous model to include asynchronous inputs.

Example: D Flip-Flop with Asynchronous Inputs

Figure 11-8 shows a model of a D flip-flop with asynchronous reset (R) and set (S) inputs and the corresponding VHDL model. The R input overrides the S input. Both signals are active low. Therefore, to set the output Q to 0, a zero pulse is applied to the reset input while the set input is held to 1 and vice versa. During synchronous operation, both S and R must be held to 1.

Example End: D Flip-Flop with Asynchronous Inputs

Now that we have seen how to create a model for a basic unit of storage with asynchronous inputs, it is relatively straightforward to create similar models for registers and counters. Such an example is presented next.

Example: Registers and Counters

We can construct a model of a typical 4-bit register composed of edge-triggered D flip-flops, using asynchronous clear and enable signals. Such a model is shown in Figure 11-9. With a few modifications, this example can be converted into a model of a counter. Rather than sampling the inputs on each clock edge, we can simply increment the value stored in the register. The initialization step can be also changed to load a preset value into the counter rather than initializing the counter to zero.

Example End: Registers and Counters

```
library IEEE;
use IEEE.std_logic_1164.all;
entity asynch_dff is
port (R, S, D, Clk : in std_logic;
      Q, Qbar : out std_logic);
end asynch_dff;

architecture behavioral of asynch_dff is
begin
output: process (R, S, Clk)
begin
if (R = '0') then
      Q <= '0' after 5 ns;
      Qbar <= '1' after 5 ns;
elsif S = '0' then
      Q <= '1' after 5 ns;
      Qbar <= '0' after 5 ns;
elsif (Clk'event and Clk = '1') then
      Q <= D after 5 ns;
      Qbar <= (not D) after 5 ns;
end if;

end process output;

end behavioral;
```

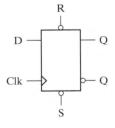

S	R	Clk	D	Q	Q
0	1	X	X	1	0
1	0	X	X	0	1
1	1	R	1	1	0
1	1	R	0	0	1
0	0	X	X	?	?

FIGURE 11-8 D flip-flop with asynchronous set and reset inputs.

```
library IEEE;
use IEEE.std_logic_1164.all;
entity reg4 is
port (D : in std_logic_vector (3 downto 0);
        Cl, enable, Clk: in std_logic;
        Q : out std_logic_vector (3 downto 0));
end reg4;


architecture behavioral of reg4 is
begin
reg_process: process (Cl, Clk)
begin
if (Cl = '1') then
        Q <= "0000" after 5 ns;
elsif (Clk'event and Clk = '1') then
        if enable = '1' then
                Q <= D after 5 ns;
        end if;
end if;

end process reg_process;

end behavioral;
```

FIGURE 11-9 A four-bit register with asynchronous inputs and enable.

Example: Asynchronous Communication

Another example of the utility of **wait** statements is the modeling of asynchronous communication between two devices. A simple four-phase protocol for synchronizing the transfer of data between a producer and consumer is shown in Figure 11-10. Let us assume that the producer (e.g., an input device such as a microphone) is providing data for a consumer device (e.g., the processor) and that the transfer of each word must be synchronized. When the producer has data to be transferred, the signal RQ is asserted. The consumer waits for a rising edge of the RQ signal before reading the data. The consumer then signals successful reception of the data by asserting the ACK signal. This causes the producer to deassert RQ, which in turn results in the consumer deasserting ACK. At this point, the transaction is completed,

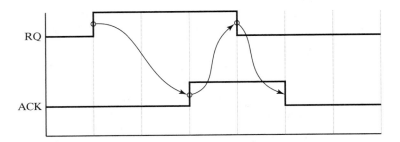

FIGURE 11-10 4-phase handshake.

and the consumer and producer can each assert that the other has successfully completed its end of the transaction. The producer and consumer can be modeled as processes that communicate via signals. Such a model is shown in Figure 11-11. Note that signals RQ, ACK, and transmit_data are declared in the architecture and are visible within both processes even though they are not in the sensitivity list of either process. Although this example is incomplete in that the processes do not perform any interesting computations with the data, it does illustrate the use of **wait** statements to control asynchronous communication between processes. Moreover, it illustrates the ability to suspend the execution of a process at multiple points within the model. Since these processes execute concurrently in simulated time, they must be capable of suspending and resuming execution at multiple points within the VHDL code. Such a model is not possible using only sensitivity lists as the mechanism for initiating process execution (although other solutions to the producer–consumer problem are possible).

Example End: Asynchronous Communication

Attributes

The example of the model of the D flip-flop introduced the idea of an attribute of a signal. Attributes can be used to return various types of information about a signal. For example, in addition to determining whether an event has occurred on a signal, we might be interested in

```vhdl
library IEEE;
use IEEE.std_logic_1164.all;

entity handshake is
port (input_data : in std_logic_vector(31 downto 0));
end handshake;

architecture behavioral of handshake is
signal transmit_data: std_logic_vector (31 downto 0);
signal RQ, ACK : std_logic;
begin

producer: process
begin
        -- wait until input data are available
        wait until input_data'event;

        -- provide data as producer
        transmit_data <= input_data;

        RQ <= '1';
        wait until ACK = '1';
        RQ <= '0';
        wait until ACK = '0';
end process producer;

consumer: process
variable receive_data : std_logic_vector (31 downto 0);
begin
        wait until RQ = '1';

        -- read data as consumer
        receive_data := transmit_data;
        ACK <= '1';
        wait until RQ = '0';
        ACK <= '0';
end process consumer;

end behavioral;
```

FIGURE 11-11 A VHDL model of the behavior shown in Figure 11-10.

knowing the amount of time that has elapsed since the last event occurred on the signal. This attribute is denoted using the following syntax:

clk'**last_event**

In effect, when the simulator executes this statement, a function call occurs that checks this property. The function returns the time since the last event occurred on signal clk. Such attributes are referred to as *function attributes*. Other useful signal attributes are shown in Table 11-1.

There are several other useful classes of attributes, but only one other class will be described here: *value attributes*. As the name suggests, these attributes return values. Some commonly used value attributes are shown in Table 11-2.

For example, the memory model shown in Figure 11-2 contains the following definition of a new type:

type mem_array **is array**(0 **to** 7) **of** std_logic_vector (31 **downto** 0);

TABLE 11-1 Some useful function signal attributes

Function Attribute	Function
signal_name'**event**	Function returning a Boolean value signifying a change in value on this signal.
signal_name'**active**	Function returning a Boolean value signifying an assignment made to this signal. This assignment may not be a new value.
signal_name'**last_event**	Function returning the time since the last event on this signal.
signal_name'**last_active**	Function returning the time since the signal was last active.
signal_name'**last_value**	Function returning the previous value of this signal.

TABLE 11-2 Some useful value attributes

Value Attribute	Value
`scalar_name`'**left**	Returns the leftmost value of `scalar_name` in its defined range.
`scalar_name`'**right**	Returns the rightmost value of `scalar_name` in its defined range.
`scalar_name`'**high**	Returns the highest value of `scalar_name` in its range.
`scalar_name`'**low**	Returns the lowest value of `scalar_name` in its range.
`scalar_name`'**ascending**	Returns true if `scalar_name` has an ascending range of values.
`array_name`'**length**	Returns the number of elements in the array `array_name`.

From Table 11-2, we have `mem_array`'**left** = 0, `mem_array`'**ascending** = true, and `mem_array`'**length** = 8. Another useful example is in the use of enumeration types. For example, when writing models of state machines described later in this chapter, it is helpful to have the following data type defined:

type `statetype` **is** (`state0,state1,state2,state3`);

In this case, we have `statetype`'**left** = `state0` and `statetype`'**right** = `state3`. This attribute is useful in behavioral models when we wish to initialize signals to values, based on their types. We may not always know the range and values of the various data types. The use of attributes makes it easy to initialize object to values without having to be concerned with the implementation. For example, on a reset operation we may simply initialize a state machine to the leftmost state of the enumerated list of possible states, that is, `statetype`'**left**.

Finally, a very useful attribute of arrays is the **range** attribute. This attribute is helpful in writing loops. For example, consider a loop that scans all of the elements in an array `value_array()`. The index range is returned by `value_array`'**range**. This attribute makes it very easy to write loops, particularly when we may not know the size of the array, as is sometimes the case when writing functions or procedures where the array size is determined when the function is called. When we do not know the array size, we can write the loop as follows:

```
for i in value_array'range loop
    ...
my_var := value_array(i);
    ...
end loop;
```

Some specific examples of the use of the range attribute can be found in the discussion of functions and procedures in Chapter 13, "Subprograms, Packages, and Libraries."

Generating Clocks and Periodic Waveforms

Since **wait** statements provide the programmer with explicit control over the reactivation of processes, they can be used for generating periodic waveforms, as shown in the following example.

Example: Generating Periodic Waveforms

We know that in a signal assignment statement we can specify several future events. For example, we might have the following signal assignment statement:

signal <= '0', '1' **after** 10 **ns**, '0' **after** 20 **ns**, '1' **after** 40 **ns**;

The execution of this statement will create the waveform shown in Figure 11-12. Now, if we place this statement within a process and use a **wait** statement, we can cause the process to be executed repeatedly, producing a periodic waveform. Recall that upon initialization of the VHDL model, all processes are executed. Therefore, every process is executed at least once. During initialization, the first set of events shown in the foregoing waveform will be produced. The execution of the **wait for** statement causes the process to be reactivated after 50 ns. This will cause the process to be executed again, generating events in the interval 50–100 ns. The process again suspends for 50 ns, and the cycle is repeated. By altering the time durations in the statement in the foregoing process, one can envision the generation of

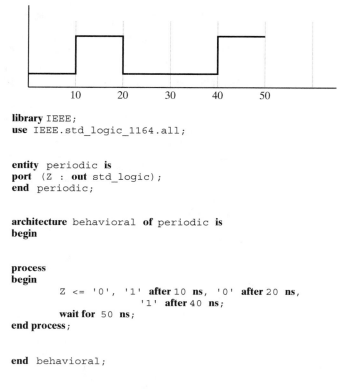

```
library IEEE;
use IEEE.std_logic_1164.all;


entity periodic is
port (Z : out std_logic);
end periodic;


architecture behavioral of periodic is
begin


process
begin
        Z <= '0', '1' after 10 ns, '0' after 20 ns,
                    '1' after 40 ns;
        wait for 50 ns;
end process;


end behavioral;
```

FIGURE 11-12 An example of the generation of periodic waveforms.

many different types of periodic waveforms. For example, if we wish to generate two-phase nonoverlapping clocks, we could use the same approach, as shown in the next example.

Example End: Generating Periodic Waveforms

Example: Generating a Two-Phase Clock

An example of a model for the generation of nonoverlapping clocks and reset pulses is shown in Figure 11-13. Such signals are very useful and are found in the majority of circuits we will come across. The reset process is a single concurrent signal assignment statement, and therefore we can dispense with the **begin** and **end** statements. Recall that CSAs are processes and we can assign them labels. Every process

```
library IEEE;
use IEEE.std_logic_1164.all;
entity two_phase is
port (phi1, phi2, reset : out std_logic);
end two_phase;

architecture behavioral of two_phase is
begin
```

```
reset_process: reset <= '1', '0' after 10 ns;
```
→ Process to generate a reset pulse

```
clock_process: process
begin
phi1 <= '1', '0' after 10 ns;
phi2 <= '0', '1' after 12 ns,
                    '0' after 18 ns;

wait for 20 ns;
end process clock_process;
```
→ Clock process

```
end behavioral;
```

FIGURE 11-13 Generation of two-phase nonoverlapping clocks.

is executed just once, at initialization. During this initialization, the reset is executed, generating a pulse of width 10 ns. Since there are no input signals or **wait** statements, the reset process is never executed again! The clock process, on the other hand, generates multiple clock edges in a 20-ns interval with each statement. Note the width of the pulses in the second clock signal: It is adjusted so as to prevent the pulses from overlapping. The **wait for** statement causes the process to be executed again 20 ns later, when each statement generates clock edges in the next 20-ns interval. This process repeats indefinitely, generating the waveforms shown in Figure 11-13. Note how concurrent signal assignment statements are mixed in with the process construct. This type of modeling using both concurrent and sequential statements is quite common. This is not surprising, since CSAs are essentially processes. If we take the viewpoint that all statements in VHDL are concurrent, then processes using sequential statements can be viewed as one complex signal assignment statement. This is a useful template to have in mind when constructing behavioral models of hardware.

Example End: Generating a Two-Phase Clock

Using Signals in a Process

We can think of processes as conventional programs that can be used in VHDL simulation models to provide us with powerful techniques for the computation of events. However, the sequential nature of processes in conjunction with the use of signals within a process can produce behavior that may be unexpected. For example, consider the circuit and corresponding model and timing behavior illustrated in Figure 10-10. Now let us enclose the concurrent signal assignment statements shown in that model in a process. This approach would represent a different model of operation for the following reason: The circuit being described is a combinational circuit; signal values are determined in a data-driven manner; signal assignment statements are executed only when input signal values change. Thus, the value of signal s3 is computed only when there is a transaction on signals s1 or In2.

Now consider the implementation using processes for which the timing is shown in Figure 11-14. When there is a change in value on either In1 or In2, the process is executed. By definition, a process executes to completion. Thus, all statements within a process are executed! Consider the value of signal s3 at initialization time when each process is executed. The value of this signal is undefined. Signal s4 has a value 1, since In1 is 0. Therefore, the value of s4 is 1 regardless of the value of s2. However, the value of s3 is undefined, and it appears as such on the trace. Now the process suspends and

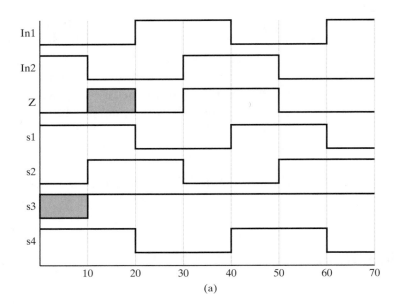

FIGURE 11-14 The effect of processes on signal assignment statements.

waits for an event on In1 or In2. It will not be executed again until 10 ns later, when a $1 \rightarrow 0$ transition occurs on In2. From the trace in Figure 11-14, we can see that forcing the process statements to be executed in order and being sensitive only to the inputs In1 and In2 produces a trace very distinct from that in Figure 10-11. Although both models were intended to represent the same circuit, we have realized different behaviors. One could make a good case that the use of a process places artificial constraints on the evaluation of signal values and that the former model is indeed a more accurate reflection of the physical behavior of the circuit. In reality, if we made the process sensitive to all of the signals (i.e., including s1, s2, s3, and s4), we would find that the process model would behave exactly like the earlier model, producing an identical trace. However, this is not a very intuitive description of the model. Suffice it to say that when using signals within a process, one must be careful that the behavior that results is indeed what the modeler had in mind.

Simulation Exercise 11.2: Use of wait Statements

This simulation exercise provides an introduction to the use of **wait** statements to suspend and resume processing under programmer control. We can use such constructs to respond to asynchronous external events. Figure 11-15 shows an example of a simple interface that reads data from an external device and buffers the data for an output device. Let us model this interface with two processes. The first process communicates with the second via a handshaking protocol such as the one demonstrated in Figure 11-10. The second process can then drive an external device such as a display.

Step 1. Using a text editor, construct a VHDL model for communication between an input process and an output process via the handshaking protocol captured in Figure 11-10. Assume that the input process can read only a single word at a time. The input process receives a single 32-bit word composed of four bytes. This word is to be transferred to an output device whose storage layout requires reversing the byte order within the word. This reversal is performed by the input process before the word is transferred to the output process, which in turn writes the value to an output port.

Step 2. Use the types `std_logic` and `std_logic_vector` for input and output signals. Declare and reference the library `IEEE` and package `std_logic_1164`.

Step 3. Create a sequence of 32-bit words as test inputs.

Step 4. Compile the model and load it into the simulator.

Step 5. Assign a delay of 10 ns for each handshake transition.

Step 6. Open a trace window and select the signals to be traced. Since we are dealing with 32-bit quantities, set the trace to display these signal values in hexadecimal notation. This format will make it considerably easier to read the values in the trace. Such commands are simulator specific.

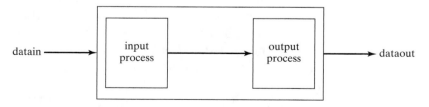

FIGURE 11-15 An example of asynchronous communication.

Step 7.   Simulate for several hundred nanoseconds.

Step 8.   Trace the four-phase handshake sequence of Figure 11-10.

Step 9.   From the trace, determine how long it takes for the input process to transfer a data item to the output process.

Step 10.   Does the rate at which the input items are provided matter? What happens as we increase the frequency with which data items are presented to the input process?

End Simulation Exercise 11.2

Modeling State Machines

The examples that have been discussed so far were combinational and sequential circuits in isolation. Processes that model combinational circuits are sensitive to the inputs, being activated whenever an event occurs on an input signal. In contrast, sequential circuits retain information stored in internal devices such as flip-flops and latches. The values stored in these devices are referred to as the *state* of the circuit. The values of the output signals may now be computed as functions of the internal state and values of the input signals. The values of the state variables may also change as a function of the input signals, but are generally updated at discrete points in time determined by a periodic signal such as the clock. With a finite number of storage elements, the number of unique states is finite, and such circuits are referred to as finite-state machines.

Figure 11-16 shows a general model of a finite-state machine. The circuit consists of a combinational component and a sequential component. The sequential component consists of memory elements, such as edge-triggered flip-flops, that record the state and are updated synchronously on the rising edge of the clock signal. The combinational component is composed of logic gates that compute two Boolean functions. The *output function* computes the values of the output signals. The *next-state function* computes the new values of the memory elements (i.e., the value of the next state).

Figure 11-16 suggests a very natural VHDL implementation using communicating concurrent processes. The combinational component

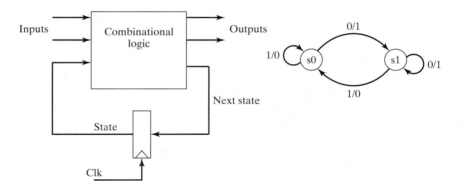

FIGURE 11-16 A behavioral model of a finite-state machine.

can be implemented within one process. This process is sensitive to events on the input signals and the state. Thus, if any of the input signals or the state variables changes value, this process is executed to compute new values for the output signals and the new state variables. The sequential component can be implemented within a second process. This process is sensitive to the rising edge of the clock signal. When it is executed, the state variables are updated to reflect the value of the next state computed by the combinational component. The VHDL description of such a state machine is shown in Figure 11-17. The model is structured as two communicating processes, with the signals state and next_state being used to communicate values between them. The structure of the process comb_process, representing the combinational component, is very intuitive. This process is constructed using a **case** statement. Each branch of the **case** represents one of the states and includes the output function and next-state function, as shown. The process clk_process updates the state variable on the rising edge of the clock. On reset, this process initializes the state machine to state state0.

There are several interesting aspects to this model. First, note the use of enumeration types for the definition of a state. The model includes the definition of a new type referred to as statetype. This type can take on the values state0 and state1 and is referred to as an *enumeration type*, since we have enumerated all possible values that a signal of this type can take—in this case, exactly two distinct

```vhdl
library IEEE;
use  IEEE.std_logic_1164.all;
entity state_machine is
port(reset, clk, x : in std_logic;
          z : out std_logic);
end state_machine;

architecture behavioral of state_machine is
type statetype is (state0, state1);
signal state, next_state : statetype := state0;
begin

comb_process: process (state, x)
begin
case state is                 -- depending upon the current state
when state0 =>                -- set output signals and next state
       if x = '0' then
              next_state <= state1;
              z <= '1';
       else   next_state <= state0;
              z <= '0';
       end if;
when state1 =>
       if x = '1' then
              next_state <= state0;
              z <= '0';
       else   next_state <= state1;
              z <= '1';
       end if;
end case;
end process comb_process;

clk_process: process
begin
-- wait until the rising edge
wait until (clk'event and clk = '1');
       -- check for reset and initialize state
       if reset = '1' then state <= statetype'left;
       else   state <= next_state;
       end if;
end process clk_process;

end behavioral;
```

FIGURE 11-17 Implementation of the state machine in Figure 11-16.

values, state0 and state1. Enumeration types enable much more readable and intuitive VHDL code. The **case** statement essentially describes the state-machine diagram in Figure 11-16. In the clock process, note how the initial state is initialized on reset. The clause statetype'**left** will return the value at the leftmost value of the enumeration of the possible values for statetype. Therefore, the initialization shown in the declaration is really not necessary. This is a common form of initialization and is also defined for other types. The default initialization value for signals is signal_name'**left**. A simulation of this state machine would produce a trace of the behavior, as shown in Figure 11-18. Note how the state labels appear in the trace, making it easier to read. Also note that the signal next_state is changing with the input signal, whereas the signal state is not. This is because state is updated only on the rising clock edge, while next_state changes whenever the input signal x changes.

The foregoing example could just as easily have been written as a single process whose execution is initiated by the clock edge. In this case, the computation of the next state, the output signals, and the state transition are all synchronized by the clock. Alternatively, we could construct a model in which outputs are computed asynchronously with the computation of the next state. Such a model is shown in Figure 11-19. This model is constructed with three processes: one each for the output function, the next-state function, and the state transition. Note how the model is constructed from the structure of the hardware: Concurrency in the circuit naturally appears as multiple concurrent processes in the VHDL model. State machines wherein the output signal values are computed only as a function of

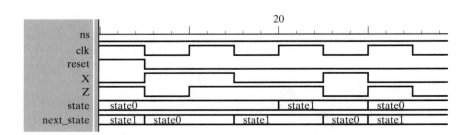

FIGURE 11-18 A trace of the operation of the state machine in Figure 11-17.

```
library IEEE;
use  IEEE.std_logic_1164.all;
entity state_machine is
port(reset, clk, x : in std_logic; z : out std_logic);
end state_machine;

architecture behavioral of state_machine is
type statetype is (state0, state1);
signal state, next_state :statetype :=state0;
begin

output_process: process (state, x)
begin
        case state is -- depending upon the current state
        when state0 => -- set output signals and next state
                if x = '1' then z <= '0'; else z <= '1'; end if;
        when state1 =>
                if x = '1' then z <= '0'; else z <= '1'; end if;
        end case;
end process output_process;

next_state_process: process (state, x)
begin
        case state is -- depending upon the current state
        when state0 => -- set output signals and next state
                if x = '1' then next_state <= state0;
                else next_state <= state1;
                end if;
        when state1 =>
                if x = '1' then next_state <= state0;
                else next_state <= state1;
                end if;
        end case;
end process next_state_process;

clk_process: process
begin
        -- wait until the rising edge
        wait until (clk'event and clk = '1');
        if reset = '1' then    state <= statetype'left;
        else state <= next_state;
        end if;
end process clk_process;

end behavioral;
```

FIGURE 11-19 Alternative model for a finite-state machine.

the current state are referred to as Moore machines. State machines wherein the output values are computed as a function of both the current state and the input values are called Mealy machines. It is evident that the aforementioned approaches to constructing state machines enable the construction of both Moore and Mealy machines by appropriately coding the output function.

Constructing VHDL Models Using Processes

A prescription for writing VHDL models using processes can now be provided. The first step is the same as that described in "Constructing VHDL Models Using CSAs" on page 123: We construct a fully annotated schematic of the system being modeled. Figure 11-20 illustrates a template for constructing such VHDL behavioral models. One approach for translating the annotated schematic to the VHDL model described in the template of Figure 11-20 is as follows:

Construct_ Process_Model

1. At this point, use of the IEEE 1164 value system is recommended. To do so, include the following two lines at the top of your model declaration:

    library IEEE;

    use IEEE.std_logic_1164.all;

    Single-bit signals can be declared to be of type std_logic, while multibit quantities can be declared to be of type std_logic_vector.

2. Select a name for the entity (entity_name), and write the entity description specifying each input and output signal port, its mode, and its associated type.

3. Select a name for the architecture (arch_name), and write the architecture description. Place both the entity and architecture descriptions in the same file.

```
library library-name-1, library-name-2;
use library-name-1.package-name.all;
use library-name-2.package-name.all;

entity entity_name is
port(    input signals  :  in type;
         output signals :  out type) ;
end entity_name;

architecture arch_name of entity_name is
```

-- declare internal signals; you may have multiple signals of
-- different types

signal *internal signals : type := initialization*;

begin

```label-1:``` **process**(-- *sensitivity list* --)
--- *declare variables to be used in the process*
variable *variable_names* : *type*:= *initialization*;
begin
-- *process body*
end process ```label-1;```
	First
	Process

```label-2:``` **process**
--- *declare variables to be used in the process*
variable *variable_names* : *type*:= *initialization*;
begin
wait until (-- *predicate*--) ;
-- *sequential statements*
wait until (-- *predicate*--) ;
-- *sequential statements*
end process ```label-2;```
	Second
	Process

internal-signal or ports <= simple, conditional, or selected CSA

-- *other processes or CSAs*

end arch_name;

FIGURE 11-20 A template for a VHDL model constructed using
CSAs and processes.

NOTE: It is a restriction of the LogicWorks package that both the entity and architecture descriptions must be in the same file. This is not a requirement of the VHDL language.

3.1 Within the architecture description, name and declare all of the internal signals used to connect the components. The architecture declaration states the type of each signal and may include initializations. The information you need is available from your fully annotated schematic.

3.2 Each internal signal is driven by exactly one component. The computation of values on each internal signal can be described using a CSA or a process.

Using CSAs

For each internal signal, select a concurrent signal assignment statement that expresses the value of the internal signal as a function of the signals that are inputs to that component. Use the value of the propagation delay through the component provided for that output signal.

Using a Process

Alternatively, if the computation of the signal values at the outputs of the component is too complex to represent using concurrent signal assignment statements, describe the behavior of the component with a process. One process can be used to compute the values of all of the output signals from that component.

3.2.1 Label the process. If you are using a sensitivity list, identify the signals that will activate the process, and place them in the sensitivity list.

3.2.2 Declare variables used within the process.

3.2.3 Write the body of the process, compute the values of output signals and the relative time at which the output signals assume these values. These output signals may be internal to the architecture or may be port signals found in the entity description. If a sensitivity list is not used, provide **wait** statements at appropriate points in the process in order to specify when the process should suspend and when it should resume execution. It is an error to have both a sensitivity list and a **wait** statement within a process.

3.3 If there are signals that are driven by more than one source, the signals must be of a resolved type. This type must have a resolution function declared for use with signals of this type. For our purposes, use the IEEE 1164 types std_logic for single-bit signals and std_logic_vector for bytes, words, or multibit quantities. These are resolved types. Make sure you provide the **library** clause and the **use** clause in order to include all of the definitions provided in the std_logic_1164 package.

3.4   If you are using any functions or type definitions provided by a third party, make sure that you have declared the appropriate library, using the **library** clause, and declared the use of the package via a **use** clause in your model.

The behavioral model will now appear structurally as shown in Figure 11-20, inclusive of both CSA and sequential statements.

Simulation Exercise 11.3: State Machines

Consider the state machine shown in Figure 11-21. This state machine has two inputs. The first is the reset signal, which initializes the machine to state 0. The second is a bit-serial input. The state machine is designed to recognize the sequence 101 in the input sequence and set the value of the output to 1. The value of the output remains at 1 until the state machine is reset.

Step 1.   Write the VHDL model for this state machine. Use an enumeration type to represent the state (i.e., the type statetype, as in Figure 11-19). Structure your state-machine description as three processes:

Process 1: Write an output process that determines the value of the single-bit output, based on the current state and the value of the single-bit input.

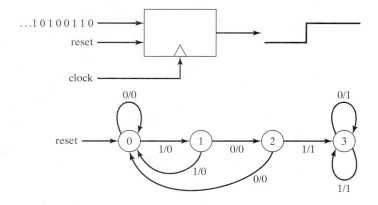

FIGURE 11-21 State machine for recognizing bit patterns.

Process 2: Write a process that computes the next state, based on the value of the input signal and the current state.

Process 3: Write a clock process that updates the state on the rising edge of the clock signal. On a `reset` pulse, the state machine is reset. Otherwise, the state is modified to reflect the next state.

Step 2. Within the simulator that you are using, structure the input stimulus as follows:

2.1 Apply a clock signal with a period of 20 ns.

2.2 Apply a reset signal that generates a single pulse of duration 30 ns.

2.3 Generate a random, bit-serial sequence with the pattern 101 embedded within the sequence.

Step 3. Simulate the model long enough to detect the pattern in the input sequence.

Step 4. Modify the model to recognize other patterns, and repeat the simulation.

Step 5. Modify the model so that after the pattern is recognized, the state machine is reinitialized to state 0. Detection of the pattern now results in a pulse on the output signal.

End Simulation Exercise 11.3

Common Programming Errors

The following are some tips for avoiding common programming errors that are made during the learning process:

Common Syntax Errors

■ Do not forget the semicolon at the end of a statement.

■ Remember it is **elsif** and not **elseif** !

■ It is an error to use **endif** instead of **end if.**

■ Do not forget to leave a space between the number and the time-base designation. For example, you should have 10 ns instead of 10ns.

- Use underscores instead of hyphens in label names—Thus, not `half-adder`, but `half_adder`.

- Expressions on the right-hand side of an assignment statement may have binary numbers expressed as x"00000000". When we use the IEEE 1164 types, even though `std_logic_vector` is a vector of bit signals, they are not of the same type as x"00000000". Simulators may thus require you to perform a type-conversion operation to convert the type of this binary number to `std_logic_vector` before you can make this assignment. The function `to_stdlogicvector`(x"00000000") is available in the package `std_logic_1164`, which is in the library `IEEE`. Check the documentation for the VHDL simulator you are using. Such type mismatches will be caught by the compiler.

Common Run-Time Errors

- It is not uncommon for programmers to use signals when they should use variables instead. Signals will be updated only after the next simulation cycle. Thus, you will find that values take effect later than you expected—for example, one clock cycle later—when this mistake has been made.

- If you use more than one process to drive a signal, the value of the signal may be undefined unless you use resolved types and have specified a resolution function. Make sure there is only one source (e.g., process) for a signal unless you mean to have shared signals. When using the `std_logic_1164` package, use `std_logic` and `std_logic_vector` types. These are resolved types that provide an associated resolution function.

- A process should have a sensitivity list or a **wait** statement.

- A process cannot have both a sensitivity list and a **wait** statement.

- Remember that all processes will be executed once when the simulation is started. This factor can sometimes cause unintended side effects if your processes are not explicitly controlled by **wait** statements.

Chapter Summary

This chapter has introduced models that use processes and sequential statements. These models are generalizations of the behavioral models with concurrent signal assignment statements described in "Simple Concurrent Signal Assignment," on page 109. The concepts introduced in this chapter include the following:

- Processes
- Sequential statements
  - ◆ if–then–else
  - ◆ case
  - ◆ loop
- **wait** statements
- Attributes
- Communicating processes
- Modeling of state machines
- Using both CSAs and processes within the same architecture description

Exercises

1. Construct a VHDL model of a parity generator for 7-bit words. The parity bit is generated in order to create an even number of bits in the word with a value of 1. Do not prescribe propagation delays to any of the components. Simulate the model, and check for functional correctness.

2. Explain why you cannot have both a sensitivity list and a **wait** statement within a process.

3. Construct and test a model of a negative-edge-triggered JK flip-flop.

4. Consider the construction of a register file with eight registers, where each register is 32 bits. Implement the model with two

processes. One process should read the register file, while the other should write the register file. You can implement the registers as signals that are declared within the architecture and therefore are visible to each process.

5. Implement a 32-bit ALU with support for the following operations: add, sub, and, or, and complement. The ALU should also produce an output signal that is asserted when the ALU output is 0. This signal may be used to implement branch instructions in a processor data path.

6. Show an example of VHDL code that transforms an input periodic clock signal to an output signal at half the frequency.

7. Construct a VHDL model for generating four-phase nonoverlapping clock signals. Pick your own parameters for pulse width and pulse separation intervals.

8. Implement and test a 16-bit up–down counter.

9. Implement and test a VHDL model for the state machine for a traffic-light controller as shown in Figure 11-22.

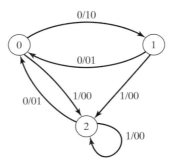

FIGURE 11-22 State machine for a traffic-light controller

10. Consider a variant of Simulation Exercise 11.3 where we are interested in the occurrence of six 1's in the bit stream. After six 1's have been detected, the output remains asserted until the state machine is reset. Construct and test this model.

12

Modeling Structure

Our model of a digital system remains that of an interconnected set of components. The preceding chapters have described how the behavior of each component could be specified in VHDL. Informally, the behavior of each component is specified as the set of output events that occurs in response to input events. Behavioral descriptions of a component may be specified using concurrent signal assignment statements. When this is infeasible because of the complexity of the event calculations, the behavioral models are specified using one or more processes and sequential statements. A third approach to describing a system is simply in terms of the interconnection of its components. In this approach, rather than focusing on what each component does, we are concerned simply with describing how components are connected. Behavioral models of each component are assumed to be provided. Such a description is referred to as a *structural model.* Such models describe only the structure of a system, without regard to the operation of individual components. This chapter discusses the construction of structural models in VHDL.

Describing Structure

A common means of conveying structural descriptions is through block diagrams. Components represented by blocks are interconnected by lines representing signals. In Chapter 10, models of a full adder using concurrent signal assignment statements were described. These models provide a description of what the system does. Instead of employing such a model, suppose we wish to describe the circuit as being constructed from two half-adders. Such a design is shown in Figure 12-1. Imagine conveying this schematic over the telephone (no faxes!) to a friend who has no knowledge of full-adder circuits. You would like to have the friend correctly reproduce the schematic as you describe it. You can also think of describing this schematic across the table to someone without showing him or her the diagram or taking a pen to paper yourself. Imagine that you could use only verbal guidelines—no pointing or gesturing with your hands! When we think of conveying descriptions in these terms, we see that we need precise and unambiguous ways to describe structure.

We might convey such a description as follows: First, we must describe the inputs and outputs to the full adder. This is not too difficult to convey verbally. We can also easily state the type and mode of

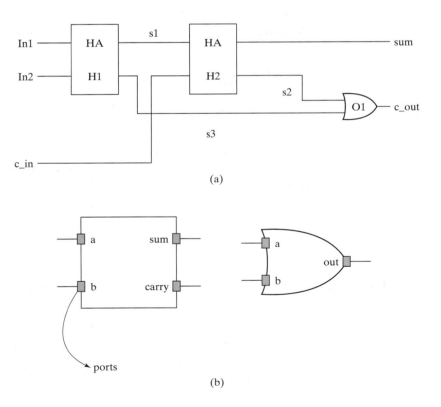

FIGURE 12-1 (a) Full-adder circuit. (b) Interface description of the half-adder and OR-gate component.

the input–output signals—for example, whether they are single-bit signals, input signals, or output signals. This information constitutes the corresponding entity description. Now imagine describing the interconnection of the components over the telephone. You would probably first list the components you need: two half-adders and a two-input OR gate. Conveying such a list of components verbally is also not difficult, but now comes the tricky part. How do you describe the interconnection of these components unambiguously? In order to do so, you must first be able to distinguish between components of the same type. For example, in Figure 12-1(a), the half-adders must be distinguished by assigning them unique labels, such as H1 and H2. The signals that will be used to connect these components are also similarly labeled. For example, we may label them s1, s2, and s3. Additional annotations that we need are the labels for the ports in a half-adder and the ports in an OR gate. Such detailed annotations are necessary so that we can refer to them unambiguously, such as the sum output port of half-adder H1.

We have now completed the schematic annotation to a point where the circuit can be described in a manner that allows the person at the other end of the telephone to draw it correctly. For example, the interconnection between H1 and H2 can be described by stating that the sum output of H1 is connected to signal s1, and the a input of H2 is connected to signal s1. Implicitly, we have stated that the sum output of H1 is connected to the a input of H2, using signal s1. We have done this indirectly by describing connections between the ports and signal s1. There is an analogy between this description and the physical process of constructing this circuit: If you were wiring this circuit on a protoboard in the laboratory, you would actually use signal wires to connect components. Once all of the components and their input and output ports are labeled, we see that we can describe this circuit in a manner that will allow our friend to correctly build the circuit.

Based on the foregoing example, we can identify a number of features that a formal VHDL structural description might possess: (i) the ability to define the list of components; (ii) the definition of a set of signals to be used to interconnect these components; and (iii) the ability to uniquely label, and therefore distinguish, between multiple copies of the same component. The VHDL syntax that realizes these features in an architecture description is shown in Figure 12-2.

```
library IEEE;
use IEEE.std_logic_1164.all;
entity full_adder is
port (In1, In2, c_in : in std_logic;
         sum, c_out : out
std_logic);

architecture structural of full_adder is
component half_adder
port (a, b: in std_logic;
         sum, carry: out std_logic);
end component;


component or_2
 port(a, b : in std_logic;
            c : out std_logic);
end component;


signal s1, s2, s3 : std_logic;
begin
H1: half_adder port map(a => In1,
            b => In2,
            sum=>s1,carry=>s3);
H2: half_adder port map(
      a => s1, b => c_in,
      sum => sum, carry => s2);
O1: or_2 port map(a => s2, b => s3,
            c => c_out);


end structural;
```

Component
Declarations

Signal
Declarations

Component
Interconnections

FIGURE 12-2 Structural model of a full adder.

The component declaration includes a list of the components being used and the input and output signals of each component, or, in VHDL terminology, the input and output ports of the component. This declaration essentially states that this architecture will be using components named `half_adder` and `or_2` gate, but so far has not stated how many of each type of component will be used. The declaration of the components is followed by the declaration of all of the signals that will be used to interconnect the components. These signals correspond to the set of signal wires you might use in the laboratory. From a programming-languages point of view, we note similarities with the manner in which we construct Basic or C++ programs. In a C++ program, for example, we declare the variables and data structures that we will use (e.g., arrays) and their types before we actually use them. In a VHDL structural model such as shown in Figure 12-2, we declare all of the components and signals that we will use before we describe how they are interconnected. Collectively, the component and signal declarations complete the declarative part of the **architecture** construct. This is analogous to the parts list that you would have if you were to build this circuit in the laboratory. Now all that remains is the process of actually "wiring" the components together. This is done in the **architecture** body that follows the declarative part and is delimited by the **begin** and **end** statements.

In considering the first statement in the **architecture** body, let us go back to our analogy of wiring the circuit on a protoboard in the laboratory. We must first acquire the components, label them, and lay them out on the board. Each component must then be connected to other components or circuit inputs, using the signal wires. Each line in the **architecture** body provides this information for each component. This is a component *instantiation* statement.

Recall that processes and concurrent signal assignments can be labeled. Components are similarly labeled. The first word, H1, is the label of a half-adder component. This word is followed by the **port map()** construct. This construct states how the input and output ports of H1 are connected to other signals and ports. The first argument of the **port map** construct simply states that the a input port of H1 is connected to the In1 port of the entity full_adder. The third argument states that the sum output port of H1 is connected to the s1 signal. The remaining **port map** constructs can be similarly interpreted. Note that both components have identical input-port names. This is not a problem, since the name is associated with a specific component that is unambiguously labeled. It is as if we were peering at the circuit through a keyhole and could see only one component at a time. We must completely describe the connections of all of the ports of each component before we can describe those of the next component. It is apparent that the interconnection of the schematic in

Figure 12-1(a) is completely specified in the structural description in Figure 12-2.

Finally, one other important feature of this model should be noted. The behavioral models of each component are assumed to be provided elsewhere; that is, there are entity–architecture pairs describing a half-adder. Note that there are no implications on the type of model used to describe the operation of the half-adder. This behavioral model could comprise concurrent signal assignment statements, use processes and sequential statements, or itself be a structural model describing a half-adder as the interconnection of gate-level behavioral models. Such hierarchies are very useful and are discussed in greater detail later in this chapter. The structural model shown in Figure 12-2 states only that a half-adder description, whose entity is labeled `half_adder`, is to be used.

Example: Structural Model of a State Machine

Consider the bit-serial adder shown in Figure 12-3(a). Two operands are applied serially, bit by bit, to the two inputs. On successive clock cycles, the combinational-logic component computes the sum and carry values for each bit position. The D flip-flop stores the carry bit between additions of successive bits and is initialized to 0. As successive bits are added, the corresponding bits of the output value are produced serially on the output signal. The state-machine diagram is shown in part (b). As described in "Modeling State Machines," on page 164, we can develop this adder as a behavioral model of a state machine that implements the state diagram shown in the figure. In this example, we show the structural model of the state-machine implementation. We have redrawn this circuit in the manner shown in Chapter 11, with a combinational-logic component and a sequential-logic component. The corresponding VHDL structural model is shown in Figure 12-4. Note the use of the **open** clause for the component labeled `D1`. The signal `qbar` at the output of the flip-flop is not used. The **port map**() clause in the component instantiation statement expresses this condition by setting the signal to **open**. The hardware analogy is that of an output pin on a chip that remains unconnected.

Example End: Structural Model of a State Machine

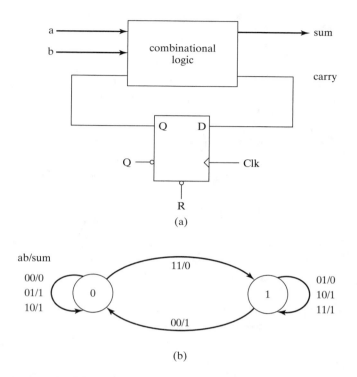

FIGURE 12-3 A bit-serial adder: (a) Logic implementation. (b) State diagram.

Constructing Structural VHDL Models

We are now ready to provide a prescription for constructing structural VHDL models. As with behavioral models, this simple methodology comprises two steps: (i) the drawing of an annotated schematic and (ii) the conversion to a VHDL model.

Construct_Structural_Schematic

1. Ensure that you have a behavioral or structural description of each component in the system being modeled. This means that you have a correct, working entity–architecture description of each component. Using the entity descriptions, create a block for each component with the input and output ports labeled.

```vhdl
library IEEE;
use IEEE.std_logic_1164.all;
entity serial_adder is
port (a, b, clk, reset : in std_logic;
         z : out std_logic);
end serial_adder;

architecture structural of serial_adder is
--
-- declare the components that we will be using
--
component comb
 port (a, b, c_in : in std_logic;
         z, carry : out std_logic);
end component;
component dff
port (clk, reset, d : in std_logic;
         q, qbar : out std_logic);
end component;
signal s1, s2 :std_logic;
begin
--
-- describe the component interconnection
--
C1: comb port map (a => a, b => b, c_in => s1,
                    z =>z, carry => s2);
D1: dff port map(clk => clk, reset =>reset, d=> s2,
                    q=>s1, qbar => open);
end structural;
```

FIGURE 12-4 VHDL structural model of the bit-serial adder.

2. Connect each port of each component to the port of another entity, or to an input or output port of the system being modeled.

3. Label each component with a unique identifier: H1, U2, and so on.

4. Label each internal signal with a unique signal name, and associate a type with this signal—for example, std_logic_vector. Make sure all of the ports connected to an internal signal and that the signals are of the same type!

5.   Label each system input port and output port, and define its mode and type.

This annotated schematic can be transcribed into a structural VHDL model. Figure 12-5 illustrates a template for writing structural models in VHDL. One approach to filling in this template is described in the next procedure. This procedure relies on the availability of the annotated schematic.

Construct_Structural_Model

1.   At this point, use of the IEEE 1164 value system is recommended. To do so, include the following two lines at the top of your model declaration:

library IEEE;

use IEEE.std_logic_1164.all;

Single-bit signals can be declared to be of type std_logic, while multibit quantities can be declared to be of type std_logic_vector.

2.   Select a name for the entity (entity_name) representing the system being modeled, and write the entity description. Specify each input and output signal port, its mode, and its associated type.

3.   Select a name for the architecture (arch_name), and write the architecture description as follows:

    3.1   Construct one component declaration for each unique component that will be used in the model. A component declaration can be easily constructed from the component's entity description.

    3.2   Within the declarative region of the architecture description—before the **begin** statement—list the component declarations.

    3.3   Following the component declarations, name and declare all of the internal signals used to connect the components. These signal names are shown on your schematic. The declaration states the type of each signal and may also provide an initial value.

    3.4   Now you can start writing the body of the architecture. For each block in your schematic, write a component instantiation statement, using the **port map**() construct. The component label is derived from the schematic. The **port map**() construct will have as many entries as there are ports on the component. Each element of the port map ( ) construct has the form

port-signal => (internal signal or entity-port)

Each port of the component is connected to an internal signal or to a port of the top-level entity. Remember, the mode and type of the port of the component must match those of the internal signal or entity port to which it is connected.

```
library library-name-1, library-name-2;
use library-name-1.package-name.all;
use library-name-2.package-name.all;
entity entity_name is
port( input signals : in type;
output signals : out type);
end entity_name;
architecture arch_name of entity_name is

-- declare components used

component component1_name
port( input signals : in type;
        output signals : out type);
end component;

component component2_name
port( input signals : in type;
        output signals : out type);
end component;

-- declare all signals used to connect components

signal internal signals : type := initialization;
begin

-- label each component and connect its ports
-- to signals or other ports

Label1: component1-name port map (port=> signal,.....);
Label2: component2-name port map (port => signal,.....);
end arch_name;
```

FIGURE 12-5 Structural-model template.

4.   Some signals may be driven from more than one source. When this is the case for a signal, the signal is a shared signal, and its type must be a resolved type. We can either define a new resolved type and its associated resolution function or simply use the IEEE 1164 data types `std_logic` and `std_logic_vector`, which are resolved types.

NOTE: Resolution functions are not supported in LogicWorks 5.

Simulation Exercise 12.1: A Structural Model

The goal of this exercise is to introduce the reader to the construction, testing, and simulation of a simple structural model.

Step 1.   Create a text file with the structural model of the full adder shown in Figure 12-2. Let us refer to this file as full-adder.vhd.

Step 2.   Create a text file with the model of the half adder shown in Figure 10-2. Let us refer to this file as half-adder.vhd. Ensure that the entity name for the half-adder in this file is the same as the name you have used for the half-adder component declaration in the full-adder structural model. Remember that the environment must have some way of being able to find and use the components that you need when you simulate the model of the full adder. Just as in the laboratory, components names are used for the purpose. In fact, the file names can be different as long as you consistently name architectures (`arch_name`), entities (`entity_name`), and components (`component_name`).

Some thought will reveal that such an approach follows intuition. Designs must be described in terms of lower level design units. File names are an artifact of the computer system we are using. When we compile an entity named `E1` in a file called homework1.vhd, we will see that compiled unit names will be based on the label `E1` rather than on homework1.vhd. This factor will enable compilation of higher level structural models to find relevant files based on the component names rather than the names of the files that they are stored in. More on the programming mechanics is discussed in Chapter 14.

Step 3.   Create a text file with a model of a 2-input OR gate. Let us refer to this file as or2.vhd. Use a gate delay of 5 ns. Again make sure that the entity name is the same as the component name for the 2-input OR gate model declared in the model of the full adder.

Step 4. Compile the files or2.vhd, half-adder.vhd, and full-adder.vhd, in this order.

Step 5. Load the simulation model into the simulator.

Step 6. Open a trace window with the signals you would like to trace. Include internal signals, which are signals that are not entity ports in the model.

Step 7. Generate a test case. Apply the stimulus corresponding to the test case to the inputs. Run the simulation for one time step. Examine the output to ensure that it is correct.

Step 8. Run the simulation for 50 ns.

Step 9. Check the behavior of the circuit, and note the timing on the internal signals with respect to the component delays.

End Simulation Exercise 12.1

Hierarchy, Abstraction, and Accuracy

The structural model of the full adder shown in Figure 12-2 presumes the presence of models of the half-adder. Although this model could be any one of the behavioral models described in Chapter 10 or Chapter 11, the model could also be a structural model itself, as shown in Figure 12-6. Thus, we have a hierarchy of models. This hierarchy can be graphically depicted as shown in Figure 12-7. Each box in the figure denotes a VHDL model: an entity–architecture pair. The architecture component of each pair may in turn reference other entity–architecture pairs. At the lowest level of the hierarchy exist architectures composed of behavioral rather than structural models of the components.

A few interesting observations can be made about the model shown in Figure 12-6. We see that structural models simply describe interconnections. They do not describe any form of behavior. There are no descriptions of how output events are computed in response to input events. How can the simulation be performed? When the structural model is loaded into the simulator, a simulation model is internally created by replacing the components by their behavioral descriptions. If the description of a component is also a structural description (as is

```
architecture structural of half_adder is
component xor2
  port (a, b : in std_logic;
            c : out std_logic);
end component;
component and2
port (a, b : in std_logic;
            c : out std_logic);
end component;
begin
EX1: xor2 port map (a => a, b => b, c => sum);
OR1: and2 port map (a=> a, b=> b, c=> carry);
end structural;
```

FIGURE 12-6 Structural model of a half-adder.

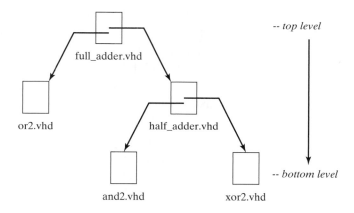

FIGURE 12-7 Hierarchy of models used in the full-adder.

the case in the model of Figure 12-2, using the architecture of the half-adder model in Figure 12-6), then the process is repeated for structural models at each level of the hierarchy. This procedure is continued until all components of the hierarchy have been replaced by behavioral descriptions. The levels of the hierarchy correspond to different levels of detail or *abstraction*. Our process is referred to as *flattening* of the hierarchy. We now have a discrete-event model that can be simulated.

From this point of view, we see that structural models are a way of managing large, complex designs. A modern design may have several million to tens of millions of gates. It is often infeasible to build a single flat simulation model at the level of individual gates to test and evaluate the complete design. This may be due to the amount of simulation time required or the amount of memory required for such a detailed model. Thus, we may chose to approximate the gate-level behavior by constructing less accurate models. For example, we have seen that a state machine may be described at the gate level or via a process-level description, as described in "Modeling State Machines," on page 164. The latter model is said to be at a higher level of abstraction. The ability to work at multiple levels of abstraction is required in order to manage large complex designs. Consider the following examples:

1. We may have a library of VHDL models of distinct components, such as those derived from the manufacturer's component data book. These models have been developed, debugged, and tested. You can construct a model of a circuit by simply using these components. The only model you will have to write is a structural model. You also have to know the component entity description so that you can correctly declare the component you are using. This approach is akin to using a library of mathematical functions in C++ or Basic.

2. After three weeks, you might have a new and improved model of a half-adder that you would like to use. You can test and debug this model in isolation. Then simply replace the old model with the new model.

Finally, we note that the simulation time is directly impacted by the level at which we construct simulation models. Consider the behavioral model of the half-adder shown in Figure 11-3. Events on input signals produce events on output signals. In contrast, when we flatten the hierarchy of Figure 12-2, events on input signals will produce events on outputs of the gates within the half-adders and eventually propagate to the output signals as events. The more detailed the model, the larger is the number of events we must expect the model to generate. The larger the number of events generated by the model, the greater is the simulation time. As a result, more accurate models will take a significantly longer time to simulate. Generally, the closer we are to making implementation decisions, the more accurate we wish the simulation to be and hence the more time is invested in simulation.

Since the full-adder model depends upon the existence of models for the half-adder and 2-input OR gate components, it follows that these models must be analyzed before the model for the full adder is analyzed. Once all of the models have been analyzed, what happens if we make changes to only some design units? Must we recompile all of the design units each time we make a change to any one? If not, what dependencies between design units must we respect? These issues are discussed in Chapter 14.

Simulation Exercise 12.2: Construction of an 8-bit ALU

The goal of this exercise is to introduce trade-offs in building models at different levels of abstraction and the effects of trading accuracy for simulation speed.

Step 1. Start with the model of a single-bit ALU as given in Simulation Exercise 10.2. This model is constructed with concurrent signal assignment statements. Replace this model with a model that replaces all of the concurrent signal assignment statements in the architecture body with sequential assignment statements and a single process. The process should be sensitive to events on input signals a, b, and c_in. The process should use variables to compute the value of the ALU output. The last statement in the process should be a signal assignment statement assigning the ALU output value to the signal result. Use a delay of 10 ns through the ALU.

Step 2. Analyze, simulate, and test this model, and ensure that all three operations (AND, OR, and add) operate correctly.

Step 3. Construct a VHDL structural model of a 4-bit ALU. Use the single-bit ALU as a building block. Use a ripple-carry implementation to propagate the carry between single-bit ALUs. Remember to compile the single-bit model before you compile the 4-bit model.

Step 4. Construct an 8-bit ALU, using the 4-bit ALU as a building block. Use a ripple-carry implementation to propagate the carry signal. Remember to compile the single-bit model before you analyze the 8-bit model.

Step 5. Based on your construction, what is the propagation delay though the 8-bit adder?

Step 6. Open a trace window with the signals you would like to trace. In this case, you will need to trace only the input and output signals in order to test the model.

Step 7. Generate a test case for each ALU operation. Apply the stimulus for a test case to the inputs. Run the simulation for a period equal to at least the delay through the 8-bit adder. Examine the output values to ensure they are correct.

Step 8. Print the trace.

Step 9. Rewrite the 8-bit model as a behavioral model rather than a structural model. In this case, there is no hierarchy of components. Use a single process and the following hints:

   9.1 Inputs, outputs, and internal variables are all now 8-bit vectors of type `std_logic_vector`. (Use the IEEE 1164 value system.)

   9.2 Make use of variables to compute intermediate results.

   9.3 Use the `case` statement to decode the opcode.

   9.4 Do not forget to set the value of the output carry signal.

   9.5 The propagation delay should be set to the delay through the hierarchical 8-bit model.

Step 10. Test the new model. You should be able to use the same inputs to test this model as you used for the hierarchical model.

Step 11. Generate a trace for the single-level model to demonstrate that the model functions correctly.

Step 12. Qualitatively compare the two models with respect to the difference in the number of events that occur in the flattened hierarchical model and the single-level model in response to a new set of inputs.

End Simulation Exercise 12.2

Generics

It is often useful to be able to parameterize models. For example, a gate-level model may have a parameterized value of the gate delay. The actual value of the gate delay is determined at simulation time by the value that is provided to the model. Having parameterized models makes it possible to construct standardized libraries of models that can be shared. The VHDL language provides the ability to construct parameterized models by using the concept of *generics*.

```
library IEEE;
use IEEE.std_logic_1164.all;

entity xor2 is
generic (gate_delay : Time := 2 ns);
port(In1, In2 : in std_logic;
          z : out std_logic);
end xor2;

architecture behavioral of xor2 is
begin
z <= (In1 xor In2) after gate_delay;
end behavioral;
```

FIGURE 12-8 An example of the use of generics.

Figure 12-8 illustrates a parameterized behavioral model of a two-input exclusive-OR gate. The propagation delay in this model is parameterized by the constant gate_delay. The default (or initialized value) value of gate_delay is set to 2 ns. This is the value of delay that will be used in simulation models such as that shown in Figure 12-6, unless a different value is specified. A new value of gate_delay can be specified at the time the model is used, as shown in Figure 12-9. This version of the half adder will make use of exclusive-OR gates that exhibit a propagation delay of 6 ns through the use of the **generic map**() construct. Note the absence of the ; after the **generic map**() construct!

The xor2 model is now quite general. Rather than manually editing and updating the delay values in the VHDL text, we can specify the value we must use when the component is instantiated. Considering the thousands of digital system components that are available, manually modifying each model when we wish to change its attributes can be quite tedious and inefficient.

Specifying Generic Values

The example in Figure 12-9 illustrates how the value of a generic constant can be specified using the **generic map**() construct when the

```
architecture generic_delay of half_adder is
component xor2
generic (gate_delay: Time); -- new value may be speci-
fied here instead
port (a, b : in std_logic;          -- of using a generic
map() construct
        c : out std_logic);
end component;
component and2
generic (gate_delay: Time);
port (a, b : in std_logic;
        c : out std_logic);
end component;
begin
EX1: xor2 generic map (gate_delay => 6 ns)
          port map(a => a, b => b, c => sum);
A1: and2 generic map (gate_delay => 3 ns)
          port map(a=> a, b=> b, c=> carry);
end generic_delay;
```

FIGURE 12-9 Use of generics in constructing parameterized models.

component is instantiated. Alternatively, the value can be specified when the component is declared. For example, in Figure 12-8, the component declaration of xor2 includes a declaration of the generic parameters. This statement can be modified to appear as follows:

generic (gate_delay:**Time**:= 6 **ns**);

Therefore, we observe that, within a structural model, there are at least two ways in which the values of generic constants of lower level components can be specified: (i) in the component declaration, and (ii) in the component instantiation statement, using the **generic map**() construct. If both ways are employed, then the value provided by the **generic map**() takes precedence. If neither is used, then the default value defined in the model is used.

The values of these generics can be passed down through multiple levels of the hierarchy. For example, suppose that the full-adder model shown in Figure 12-2 defines the value of gate_delay for all lower level modules. In this case, the half-adder module may be modified to appear as shown in Figure 12-10.

```
library IEEE;
use IEEE.std_logic_1164.all;

entity half_adder is
generic (gate_delay:Time:= 3 ns);
port (a, b : in std_logic;
            sum, carry : out std_logic);
end half_adder;

architecture generic_delay2 of half_adder is
component xor2
generic (gate_delay: Time);
 port(a,b : in std_logic;
            c : out std_logic);
end component;

component and2
generic (gate_delay: Time);
port (a, b : in std_logic;
      c : out std_logic);
end component;

begin
EX1: xor2 generic map (gate_delay => gate_delay)
        port map(a => a, b => b, c => sum);
A1: and2 generic map (gate_delay => gate_delay)
        port map(a=> a, b=> b, c=> carry);
end generic_delay2;
```

FIGURE 12-10 Passing values of generics through multiple levels of the hierarchy.

Within the half-adder, the default gate delay is set to 3 ns. This is the value of gate_delay that is normally passed into the lower level models for xor2 and and2. However, if the full-adder description uses **generic map**s to provide new values of the gate delay to the half-adder models that are instantiated in the structural description shown in Figure 12-2, then these values take precedence and will flow down to the gate-level models. This process is depicted graphically in Figure 12-11. From the figure, it is evident that by changing the value

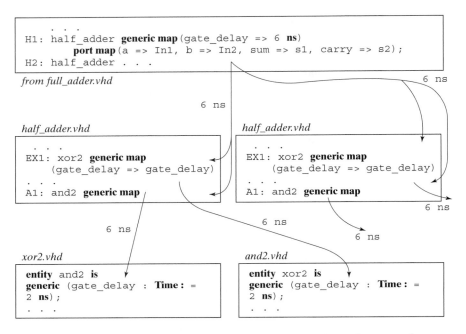

```
              . . .
      H1: half_adder generic map(gate_delay => 6 ns)
               port map(a => In1, b => In2, sum => s1, carry => s2);
      H2: half_adder . . .
```

from full_adder.vhd

half_adder.vhd   *half_adder.vhd*

```
       . . .                                          . . .
EX1: xor2 generic map                         EX1: xor2 generic map
     (gate_delay => gate_delay)                    (gate_delay => gate_delay)
       . . .                                          . . .
A1: and2 generic map                          A1: and2 generic map
```

xor2.vhd   *and2.vhd*

```
entity and2 is                                entity xor2 is
generic (gate_delay : Time: =                 generic (gate_delay : Time: =
2 ns);                                        2 ns);
 . . .                                         . . .
```

FIGURE 12-11 Parameter passing through the hierarchy, using generics.

of `gate_delay` in the full-adder model, you can cause the gate-level VHDL models for `xor2` and `and2` to use this value of the gate delay in the simulation. Although the models are written with default gate-delay values of 2 ns, the new value overrides this default value.

Some Rules for Using Generics

The terminology is quite appropriate: The use of generics enables us to write *generic* models whose behavior in a particular simulation is determined by the value of the generic parameters. Generics appear very much like ports. They are a part of the interface specification of the component. However, unlike ports, they do not have a physical interpretation. They are more a means of conveying information through the design hierarchy, thereby enabling component designs to be parameterized. Generics are constant objects. Therefore, they cannot be written, but only read. The values of generic parameters must be computable at the time the simulator is loaded with the VHDL model. Therefore, we may include expressions in the value of a generic parameter. However, the value of this expression must be computable at the time the simulator is loaded. Finally, we must be careful about the precedence of the values of generic objects, as described in the preceding sections. The following examples further illustrate the power of constructing parameterized models.

Example: N-*Input OR gate*

One class of generic gate-level models is such that the number of inputs can be parameterized. Therefore, we can have just one VHDL model of an *N*-input gate. We can produce a 2, 3, or 6 input gate model by simply setting the value of a generic parameter. This example is shown in Figure 12-12. When this OR-gate model is used in a VHDL model, the generic parameter n must be mapped to the required number of inputs, using the **generic map()** construct in a higher level structural model. For example, if we were using several OR gates in a structural model, we would have one instantiation

```
library IEEE;
use IEEE.std_logic_1164.all;
entity generic_or is
generic (n: positive:=2);
port (in1 : in std_logic_vector ((n-1) downto 0);
         z : out std_logic);
end generic_or;

architecture behavioral of generic_or is
begin
process (in1)
variable sum : std_logic:= '0';
begin
sum := '0'; -- on an input signal transition sum
must be reset to 0
for i in 0 to (n-1) loop
sum := sum or in1(i);
end loop;
z <= sum;
end process;
end behavioral;
```

FIGURE 12-12 An example of a parameterized gate-level model.

statement for each model. Each instantiation statement would include the following statement:

generic map (n=>3);

In this statement, the value 3 would be replaced by the number of inputs for that particular gate. Note that there is only one VHDL model. The conventional-programming-language analogy would be that of using functions where the arguments determine the computation performed by the function.

Example End: N-*Input OR gate*

Example: N-*Bit Register*

Another example of the use of generics is a parameterized model of an *N*-bit register. Generics may be used to configure the model in a specific instance to be of a fixed number of bits. Let us consider a register composed of D flip-flops with asynchronous reset and load enable signals. The model is shown in Figure 12-13. The operation of the register (process) is sensitive to the occurrence of an event on the `reset` or `clk` signals. The size of the register is determined when this model is instantiated by a higher level model. The default value is a 2-bit register. Note how the value of `q` is set using the **others** construct. Since `q` is a vector of bits, this statement provides a concise approach to specifying the values of all the bits in a vector when they are equal. A trace of the operation of this 2-bit register in the presence of various waveforms on the input signals is shown in Figure 12-14.

Example End: N-*bit Register*

Simulation Exercise 12.3: Use of Generics

This exercise illustrates the utility of the use of generics for parameter passing in structural models.

Step 1.   Start with the model of the single-bit ALU written using CSAs from Simulation Exercise 10.2. Modify this model to include a generic parameter to specify the gate delay. Set the default gate delay to 3 ns. Use 2 ns for the delay through the multiplexor.

```
library IEEE;
use IEEE.std_logic_1164.all;
entity generic_reg is
generic (n: positive:=2);
port ( clk, reset, enable : in std_logic;
       d : in std_logic_vector (n-1 downto 0);
       q : out std_logic_vector (n-1 downto 0));
end generic_reg;

architecture behavioral of generic_reg is
begin
reg_process: process (clk, reset)
begin
  if reset = '1' then
      q <= (others => '0');
  elsif (clk'event and clk = '1') then
      if enable = '1' then
          q <= d;
      end if;
    end if;
  end process reg_process;
  end behavioral;
```

FIGURE 12-13 An example of a parameterized model of an *N*-bit register.

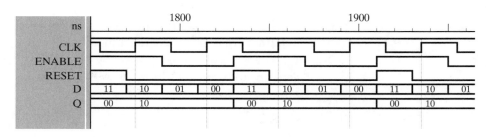

FIGURE 12-14 Trace of the operation of a 2-bit register.

Step 2. Compile, simulate, and test this model, and ensure that all three operations (AND, OR, and add) are correctly computed using this value of the gate delay.

Step 3. Construct a VHDL structural model of a 2-bit ALU. Use the single-bit ALU as a building block. Use a ripple-carry implementation to propagate the carry between single-bit ALUs. Remember to analyze (compile) the single-bit model before you analyze (compile) the 2-bit model.

Step 4. Use the **generic map** () construct in the structural model of the 2-bit ALU to set the value of the gate delay for the OR gates to 4 ns and for the AND gates to 2 ns.

Step 5. Compile, simulate, and verify the functionality of this model.

Step 6. Open a trace window with the signals you would like to trace. In this case, you will need to only trace the input and output signals in order to test the model.

Step 7. Note how easy it is to modify the values of the gate delay at the top level. Now change the model to use a generic *N*-input AND gate. The model can be modified as follows:

    7. 1 Modify the model of the AND gate to follow the model shown in Figure 12-12.

    7. 2 Modify the single-bit ALU model to include a generic parameter specifying a default value of 3 for the number of inputs to the AND gate.

    7. 3 In the model of the single-bit ALU, declare the generic AND model as a component, and replace the CSA describing the operation of the AND gate with a component instantiation statement for the generic AND model. This instantiation statement should also include a **generic map** () statement providing the number of gate inputs as a parameter.

    7. 4 Since the default value of the number of inputs to the AND gate is 3, you must pass parameters correctly in order for this model to function.

Step 8. Compile and test your model. Trace the input and output signals to determine that the model functions correctly.

Step 9. Experiment with other possibilities. For example, you can use a generic model of an OR gate as well. This model is shown in Figure 12-12.

End Simulation Exercise 12.3

Common Programming Errors

The following are some common programming errors:

- Generics can have their values defined at three places: within the model, in a component instantiation statement using the **generic**

map() construct, and within an architecture in a component declaration. Changing the value of the generics in one place may not have the intended effect, because of precedence of the other declarations. The actual value of the generic parameter thus may not be what you expect.

■ When using default bindings of components, the name, type, and mode of each signal in the component declaration must exactly match those of the entity; otherwise, an error will result.

■ Inheriting a generic value by way of default intializations in the component declarations in the higher level may lead to unexpected values of the generic parameters. A clear idea of how generic values are propagated through the hierarchy is necessary in order to ensure that the acquired values of the generic parameters correspond to the intended values.

Chapter Summary

The focus of this chapter has been on the ability to specify hierarchical models of digital systems, *ignoring* how the internal behavior of components may be specified. Internal behavior can be described using language features described in Chapter 10 and Chapter 11. An important aspect of the construction of hierarchical models is the ability to construct parameterized behavioral models and to be able to determine values of parameters by passing information down this hierarchy. This functionality is facilitated by the **generic** construct and enables the construction of libraries of models that can be shared by designers.

The concepts covered in this chapter include

■ Structural models
   ◆ component declaration
   ◆ component instantiation
■ Construction of hierarchical models
   ◆ abstraction
   ◆ trade-offs between accuracy and simulation speed

- Generics
  - ◆ specifying generic values
  - ◆ constructing parameterized models

We now have command of the basic constructs for creating VHDL models of digital systems. The upcoming chapters address remaining issues in support of these basic constructs in order to provide a complete set of modeling tools.

Exercises

1. Complete the structural model of the bit-serial adder shown in Figure 12-4 by constructing a model for the two components. You must complete the design of the combinational-logic component. Compile, simulate, and test the model.

2. Consider the detailed hierarchical model of the 8-bit ALU constructed in Simulation Exercise 12.2. Now consider a single-level behavioral model of the 8-bit ALU constructed using a single process and 8-bit data types. Compare the two models, and comment on the differences in simulation accuracy, simulation time, and functionality.

3. You are part of a software group developing algorithms for processing speech signals for a new digital-signal-processing chip. To test your software, your options are to construct (i) a detailed hierarchical model of the chip, composed of gate-level models at the lowest level of the hierarchy, or (ii) a behavioral-level model of the chip that can implement the algorithms that you wish to use. Your goal is to produce correct code for a number of algorithms prior to detailed testing on a hardware prototype. How would you evaluate these choices, and what are the trade-offs in picking one approach over the other?

4. Construct and test a structural model of the circuit shown in the accompanying figure. Note that there are many different ways in which to do this. You might consider each gate as a component, or each group of gates as a component represented by the Boolean function that is computed by the gates.

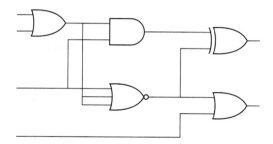

5. Consider the circuit shown below. Construct a structural model composed of two components: a generic *N*-input AND gate and a two-input OR gate. By passing the appropriate generic value, we can instantiate the same basic AND gate component as a two-input or three-input AND gate.

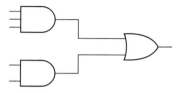

6. Use generics to set default gate delays for the components in Exercise 5. Now instantiate each AND gate with different gate delays, using the **generic map** () construct.

7. Modify the generic model of the *N*-bit register shown in Figure 12-13 to operate as a counter that is initialized to a preset value.

13

Subprograms, Packages, and Libraries

With any large body of software, we need mechanisms for structuring programs, reusing software modules, and otherwise managing design complexity. In conventional programming languages, mechanisms for doing so have been available to us for some time. The VHDL language also provides support for such mechanisms through the definition and use of procedures and functions for encapsulating commonly used operations. However, the presence of the **signal** class of objects, the fact that the programs represent the discrete-event simulation of physical systems, and the notion of simulation time generate considerations that do not arise for their counterparts in conventional programming languages. For example, where are procedures declared and used? Can **wait** statements be used in a procedure? How are signals passed and modified? Can functions operate on signals? The essential issues governing the use of functions and procedures are initially discussed in this chapter.

Related groups of functions and procedures can be aggregated into a module that can be shared across many different VHDL models. Such a module is referred to as a *package*. In addition to the definitions of procedures and functions, packages may contain user-defined data types and constants and can be placed in *libraries*. Libraries are repositories for design units in general, and packages are a type of design unit. Collectively, procedures, functions, packages, and libraries provide facilities for creating and maintaining modular and reusable VHDL programs.

Essentials of Functions

As in traditional programming languages, functions are used to compute a value based on the values of the input parameters. An example of a function declaration is

> **function** rising_edge (**signal** clock:**in** std_logic) **return≠boolean**;

The function definition specifies the function name, the input parameters, and the type of the result. Functions return values that are computed using the input parameters. Therefore, we would expect that the parameter values are used, but not changed within the function. This notion is captured in the *mode* of the parameter. Parameters of mode **in** can only be read. Functions cannot modify parameter values (procedures can), and therefore functions do not have any parameters of mode **out**. Since the mode of all function parameters is **in**, we do not have to specify the mode of a parameter. A discussion of other modes is presented in "Essentials of Procedures," on page 210.

Consider the structure of a function as shown in Figure 13-1. The function has a name (rising_edge) and a set of parameters. The parameters in the function definition are referred to as *formal* parameters. Formal parameters can be thought of as placeholders that describe the type of object that will be passed into the function. When the function is actually called in a VHDL module, the arguments in the call are referred to as *actual* parameters. For example, the above function may be called in the following manner:

> rising_edge (enable);

In this case, the actual parameter is the signal enable, and it takes the place of the formal parameter clock in the body of the function.

```
function rising_edge (signal clock: std_logic) return boolean
is
--
--declarative region: declare variables local to the
function
--
begin
-- body
--
return (expression)
end rising_edge;
```

FIGURE 13-1 Structure of a function.

The type of the formal and actual parameters must match—except for formal parameters that are constants. In this case, the actual parameter may be a variable, signal, constant, or an expression. When no class is specified, the default class of the parameter is a constant. **Wait** statements are not permitted in functions. Thus, functions execute in zero simulation time. It follows that **wait** statements cannot exist in any procedures called by a function (although procedures are allowed to have **wait** statements). Furthermore, as parameters are restricted to be of mode **in**, functions cannot modify the input parameters. Thus, signals passed into functions cannot be assigned values. This behavior is consistent with the conventional definition of functions.

Example: Detection of Signal Events

Often, we find it useful to perform simple tests on signals to determine whether certain events have taken place. For example, the detection of a rising edge is common in the modeling of sequential circuits. Figure 13-2 shows the VHDL model of a positive edge triggered D flip-flop similar to one we have discussed previously. The only difference is the inclusion of a function for testing for the rising edge, rather than having the corresponding code in the body of the VHDL description. Note the placement of the function in the declarative portion of the architecture. Normally, this region is used to declare signals and constants used in the body of the code. Therefore, we might expect that we can also declare functions (or procedures) that are used in the architecture, too. This is indeed the case. The function could have also been declared in the declarative region of the process that called the function (i.e., between the keywords **process** and **begin**). The question is whether you wish to have the function be visible to, and therefore callable from, all processes in the architecture body, or visible to just one process. In practice, we would much rather place related functions and procedures in packages, a type of design unit described later in this chapter. In fact, such a function is provided in the package `std_logic_1164`.

Example End: Detection of Signal Events

```vhdl
library IEEE;
use IEEE.std_logic_1164.all;
entity dff is
port (D, Clk : in std_logic;
          Q, Qbar : out std_logic);
end dff;


architecture behavioral of dff is
function rising_edge (signal clock : std_logic) return
boolean is
variable edge : boolean := FALSE;
begin
edge := (clock = '1' and clock'event);
return (edge);
end rising_edge;

begin
output: process
begin
wait until (rising_edge(Clk));

   Q <= D after 5 ns;
       Qbar <= not D after 5 ns;

end process output;
end behavioral;
```

FIGURE 13-2 An example of the use of functions.

Type-Conversion Functions

Type conversion is another common instance of the use of functions. The model of the memory module in "The Process Construct," on page 135, represented memory as a one-dimensional array. This array was indexed by an integer. However, memory addresses are provided as an *N*-bit binary address. We find that we need to convert this bit vector representing the memory address to an integer used to index the array representing memory. In other instances, we may want to use models of components developed by others. However, let's say that others have used signals of type **bit** and **bit_vector**, while you have been using signals of type std_logic and std_logic_vector. If it is possible (and correct) to use their models, type-conversion functions will be necessary for interoperability if we do not wish to invest in the time to convert their models to use the IEEE 1164 types.

Example: Type Conversion

Consider the VHDL type **bit_vector** and the IEEE 1164 type std_logic_vector. We may wish to make assignments from a variable of one type to a variable of the other type. For example, consider the VHDL model of the memory system shown in "The Process Construct," on page 135. In this model, we use the function to_stdlogicvector() that is provided in the package std_logic_1164.vhd (more on this package in "Essentials of Packages," on page 219). This function takes as an argument an object of type **bit_vector** and returns a value of type std_logic_vector. Conversely, we may wish to convert from **bit_vector** to std_logic_vector. An example of the implementation of this function is shown in Figure 13-3. The function simply scans the vector and converts each element of the input std_logic_vector. The type **bit** may take on values 0 and 1, whereas the type std_logic may take on one of nine values. Note the declaration of the variable outvalue. The function declaration does not provide the size of the number of bits in the argument. This size is set when the formal parameter is associated with the actual parameter at the time the function is called. In this case, how can we declare the size of any local variable that is to have the same number of bits as the input parameter? The answer is by using attributes. As discussed previously, arrays have an attribute named **length**. The value of svalue'**length** is the length of the array. By using unconstrained arrays in the definition of the function, we can realize a flexible function implementation where the actual sizes of the parameters are determined when the actual parameters are bound to formal parameters, which occurs when the function is called.

There are many ways in which to perform such conversions, and Figure 13-3 shows but one of them. By examining commercial packages such as std_logic_arith.vhd and std_logic_1164.vhd,

```
function to_bitvector (svalue : std_logic_vector) return
bit_vector is
variable outvalue : bit_vector (svalue'length-1 downto 0);
begin
for i in svalue'range loop -- scan all elements of the array
case svalue (i) is
when '0' => outvalue (i) := '0';
when '1' => outvalue (i) := '1';
when others => outvalue (i) := '0';
end case;
end loop;
return outvalue;
end to_bitvector
```

FIGURE 13-3 An example of a type-conversion function.

we will find many such conversion functions. Examples include conversion from `std_logic_vector` to **integer** and vice-versa.

Example End: Type Conversion

Essentials of Procedures

Procedures are subprograms that can modify one or more of the input parameters. The following procedure declaration illustrates the procedure interface:

procedure read_v1d (**variable** f:**in text**;v :**out** std_logic_vector);

This is a procedure to read data from a file, where f is a file parameter. The first characteristic we might notice is that parameters may be of mode **out**. Just as parameters of mode **in** must be read and cannot be written, parameters of mode **out** cannot be read and used in a procedure, but can only be written. We may also have parameters of mode **inout**, which may be both read and written. As with functions, the type of the formal parameters in a procedure declaration must match the type of the actual parameters that are used when the procedure is called. If the class of the procedure parameter is not explicitly declared, then parameters of mode **in** are assumed to be of class **constant**, while parameters of mode **out** or **inout** are assumed to be of class **variable**. Variables declared within a procedure are initialized on each call to the procedure, and their values do not persist across invocations of the procedure.

Example: Interface to Memory

Let us consider a VHDL model for a simple processor for which we have two components: a CPU and memory. The behavioral model of the CPU must be able to read and write locations from memory. These operations are common candidates for implementation as procedures. We will create two procedures: one to read and one to write memory locations. We will assume the memory model and associated signals as shown in "Modeling a Memory Module," on page 136, with the addition of one additional signal from memory that signifies the completion of a memory operation. These procedures are shown in Figure 13-4. Both procedures should manipulate the signals shown in the memory interface in Figure 11-1. There are a number of interesting features shown here. First, note the presence of **wait** statements within the procedure. Thus, a process can suspend inside a procedure. Furthermore, signals can be assigned values within a procedure. This raises the issue of how signals are passed into a procedure, and this issue is dealt with momentarily. Signals that are modified within the procedure are declared to be of mode **out**. For example, see signal R in procedure `mread()` in Figure 13-4.

The body of the architecture description is likely to include processes within which the procedure calls can be made. Alternatively, the procedures could have been declared within the declarative region of the process—just before the **begin** statement and after the **process** statement. Just as processes can declare and use variables that are local to the process, processes may also declare and use procedures within a process. However, in this case, they would be visible only within that process.

Example End: Interface to Memory

```
library IEEE;
use IEEE.std_logic_1164.all;
entity CPU is
port ( DI : out std_logic_vector ( 31 downto 0);
       ADDR :out std_logic_vector (2 downto 0);
       R, W : out std_logic;
       DO : in std_logic_vector(31 downto 0);
       S : in std_logic);
end CPU;

architecture behavioral of CPU is
procedure mread (address : in std_logic_vector (2 downto
0);
signal R : out std_logic;
signal S : in std_logic;
signal ADDR : out std_logic_vector (2 downto 0);
signal data : out std_logic_vector (31 downto 0)) is
begin
ADDR <= address;
R <= '1';
wait until S = '1';
data <= DO;
R <= '0';
end mread;

procedure mwrite (
        address : in std_logic_vector (2 downto 0);
        signal data : in std_logic_vector (31 downto 0);
        signal ADDR : out std_logic_vector (2 downto 0);
        signal W : out std_logic;
        signal DI : out std_logic_vector (31 downto 0)) is
begin
ADDR <= address;
W <= '1';
wait until S = '1';
DI <= data;
W <= '0';
end mwrite;
--
-- any signal declarations for the architecture here
--
```

FIGURE 13-4 An example of the use of procedures.

```
begin
--
-- CPU behavioral description here
process
begin
--
-- behavioral description
--
end  process;

process
begin
--
-- behavioral description
--
end  process;
end behavioral;
```

FIGURE 13-4 (cont.)

Using Procedures

Signals cannot be declared within procedures. However, signals can be passed into procedures as parameters. Due to visibility rules, procedures can make assignments to signals that are not explicitly declared in the parameter list. For example, procedures declared within a process can make assignments to signals corresponding to the ports of the encompassing entity. This is possible because the ports are visible to the process. The procedure is said to have side effects, since it has an effect on a signal that is not declared in the parameter list. This approach is poor programming practice, however, since it makes it difficult to reason about the models (e.g., when debugging) and understand their behavior. Clarity and understanding of the code is enhanced if parameters are passed explicitly rather than relying on side effects. If the class of a parameter is not declared and the mode is **out** or **inout**, then the class defaults to that of a variable. If the mode is **in**, the class of the parameter defaults to a constant.

Procedures can also be placed in the declarative region of a process. We know that process bodies cannot have both a sensitivity list and a **wait** statement. Therefore, when we use procedures, it follows that a process that calls a procedure with a **wait** statement cannot have a sensitivity list.

Concurrent and Sequential Procedure Calls

Depending on how procedures are used, we can distinguish between concurrent and sequential procedure calls. Remember the concurrent signal assignment statements from "Simple Concurrent Signal Assignment," on page 109? Each statement represented the assignment of a value to a signal, and this assignment occurred in simulated time simultaneously with the execution of the other concurrent signal assignment statements and processes. Concurrent procedure calls can be viewed similarly. The procedure is invoked in the body of an architecture simultaneously with other concurrent procedures, concurrent signal assignment statements, or processes. The procedure is invoked when there is an event on a signal that is an input parameter to the procedure. It follows that if we use a concurrent procedure, the parameter list cannot include a variable, since variables cannot exist outside of a process. In contrast, sequential procedure calls are calls where the procedure is invoked within the body of a process. In this case, the invocation of the procedure is determined by the sequence of execution of statements within the process—just as in a conventional program. The following example should help solidify our understanding of the differences between concurrent and sequential procedure calls.

Example: Concurrent and Sequential Procedure Calls

Figure 13-5 illustrates an example of a concurrent procedure call. The structural model of a bit-serial adder from Figure 12-3 has been rewritten such that the D flip-flop component instantiation statement has been replaced by a procedure. The procedure is invoked concurrently with the component `comb` whenever there are events on the signals that are declared to be of mode **in**. Thus, events on the `clk`, `reset`, or `d` inputs will cause this procedure to be invoked. From the procedure body, we see that the output is modified only on the rising edge of the `clk` signal.

```vhdl
library IEEE;
use IEEE.std_logic_1164.all;
entity serial_adder is
port (a, b, clk, reset : in std_logic;
            z : out std_logic);
end serial_adder;

architecture structural of serial_adder is
component comb
  port (a, b, c_in : in std_logic;
            z, carry : out std_logic);
end component;

procedure dff(signal d, clk, reset : in std_logic;
                              signal q, qbar : out std_logic) is
begin
if (reset = '0') then
        q <= '0' after 5 ns;
        qbar <= '1' after 5 ns;
      elsif (clk'event and clk = '1') then
      q <= d after 5 ns;
      qbar <= (not D) after 5 ns;
 end if;
end dff;

signal s1, s2 : std_logic;

begin
C1: comb port map (a => a, b => b, c_in => s1, z =>z, carry
=> s2);
--
-- concurrent procedure call
--
dff(clk => clk, reset =>reset, d=> s2, q=>s1, qbar
=>open);
end structural;
```

FIGURE 13-5 An example of a concurrent procedure

This structure does appeal to our understanding of VHDL programs. Consider what would happen in the model in the example of Figure 12-4. When this model is simulated, let us assume that the component dff would be replaced by a behavioral model similar to the one shown in Figure 11-7. We see that the procedure effectively implements the same behavior. Note how the parameter list explicitly associates the formal and actual parameters rather than having this association made by virtue of the position in the call. The signal qbar is associated with the keyword **open** in the procedure call. This approach is akin to leaving a pin of a device (dff) unconnected.

Figure 13-6 shows the equivalent implementation as a sequential procedure call. The procedure is encased in a process with an explicit **wait** statement. Note the structure of the **wait** statement. If an event occurs on any of the signals in the list, the process will be executed, which in this case will cause the procedure dff() to be called. This procedure-call model is equivalent to the model shown in Figure 13-5.

Example End: Concurrent and Sequential Procedure Calls

Subprogram and Operator Overloading

A very useful feature of the VHDL language is the ability to *overload* the subprogram name. For example, there are several models and implementations of a D flip-flop. We saw a few examples in "The **wait** Statement," on page 148. Imagine that we want to write behavioral models of sequential circuits that include D flip-flops. We might be using procedures such as the one shown in Figure 13-5 to model the behavior of a D flip-flop. If we wish to incorporate models that have asynchronous set and clear signals, we might write another procedure with a different name, say, asynch_dff(). What if we wish to have procedures that operate on signal arguments of type **bit_vector** rather than std_logic_vector? We would then have to write distinct procedures to incorporate models with these types and behaviors. By accommodating various possibilities of argument types and flip-flop behavior, we might have to write many different procedures while keeping track of the names to distinguish them.

```
library IEEE;
use IEEE.std_logic_1164.all;
entity serial_adder is
port (a, b, clk, reset : in std_logic;
            z : out std_logic);
end serial_adder;

architecture structural of serial_adder is
component comb
  port (a, b, c_in : in std_logic;
            z, carry : out std_logic);
end component;
procedure dff(signal d, clk, reset : in std_logic;
                signal q, qbar : out std_logic) is
begin
 if (reset = '0') then
        q <= '0' after 5 ns;
        qbar <= '1' after 5 ns;
      elsif (clk'event and clk = '1') then
      q <= d after 5 ns;
      qbar <= (not D) after 5 ns;
 end if;
end dff;
signal s1, s2 : std_logic;
begin
C1: comb port map (a => a, b => b, c_in => s1, z =>z,
carry => s2);
process
begin
 dff(clk => clk, reset =>reset, d=> s2, q=> s1, qbar =>
open);
wait on clk, reset, s2;
end process;
end structural;
```

FIGURE 13-6 An example of a sequential procedure call.

It would be very helpful to be able to use a single name for all procedures describing the behavior of various types of D flip-flops. We would like to call dff(), for instance, with the right parameters and let the compiler determine which procedure to use, based on the number and type of arguments. For example, consider the two procedure calls

```
dff(clk,d,q,qbar)
```
and
```
dff(clk,d,q,qbar,reset,clear)
```

From the arguments, we can see that we are referring to two different procedures, one that uses asynchronous reset and clear inputs and one that does not (e.g., corresponding to Figure 11-8 and Figure 11-7, respectively). From the type and number of arguments, we can tell which procedure we meant to use. This process is referred to as overloading subprogram names, or simply *subprogram overloading*. When we create such a set of procedures or functions with overloaded names, we would probably place them in a package and make the package contents visible via the **use** clause. If we examine the contents of some of the packages shown in the VHDL reference manual provided in electronic form with the software, we will see examples of overloaded functions and subprograms. For example, note that in `std_logic_1164.vhd`, the Boolean functions **and**, **or**, etc., have been defined for the type `std_logic`.

NOTE: Operator overloading is not implemented in LogicWorks 5. This section is for informational purposes only.

Similarly, the operators such as * and + have been defined for certain predefined types of the language such as integers. What if we wish to perform such operations on other data types that we may create? We can overload these operators by providing definitions of * and + for these new data types. CAD tool vendors typically distribute packages that contain definitions of operators and subprograms for various operations on data types that are not predefined for the language. For example, the `std_logic_arith.vhd` package distributed by CAD tool vendors provides definitions for various operators over the `std_logic` and `std_logic_vector` types. Two examples of overloading the definitions of * and + operators taken from this package are as follows:

function "*"(arg1,arg2 : std_logic_vector) **return**
std_logic_vector;
function "+"(arg1,arg2 :signed) **return** signed;

These statements mean that if the contents of this package are included in a model via the **use** clause, then statements such as

```
s1 <= s1 + s2;
```

are valid, where all three signals are of type `std_logic`. Otherwise, the + operation is not defined for objects of type `std_logic`, and this statement would be in error.

Procedures and functions are necessary constructs for building reusable blocks of VHDL code, for hiding design complexity, and for managing large complex designs. As we have seen in this section, they are also a means for enriching the language in order to easily handle new data types by encapsulating the definitions of common operations and operators over these data types. Even with a small number of new data types, the need to overload all of the common operators can generate quite a large number of functions. Furthermore, when we think of overloading subprogram names, we can generate quite a few additional procedures or functions. Packages are a mechanism for structuring, organizing, and using such user-defined types and subprograms. These concepts are discussed next.

Essentials of Packages

As we acquire larger groups of functions and procedures within the models that we construct, we must consider how they will be used. We can use text editors and manually insert these functions into the VHDL models as we use them. This is a rather tedious process at best, however, especially when the models we construct grow large. A better approach would be to group logically related sets of functions and procedures into a module that can be easily shared among distinct designs and people. *Packages* are a means for doing so within the VHDL language.

Packages provide for the organization of type definitions, functions, and procedures so that they can be shared across distinct VHDL programs. To gain an intuition for the constructs used in building packages, it is instructive to consider how we try to reuse code modules across projects. When we are working on large class projects, we attempt to make the most efficient use of our time by reusing functions or procedures that we may have written for older programs, have found somewhere on the Internet, or have garnered from friends. For example, imagine that you have painstakingly put together a package that contains useful functions, procedures, and data types to help designers build simulation models of common computer architectures. This package may include definitions of new types for registers, instructions, and memories, as well as procedures for reading or writing memories, procedures for performing logical-shift operations, and functions for type-conversion operations. After months of tedious development, you are now interested in promoting its use among fellow VHDL developers. How might you communicate the contents of this package in convincing them of its utility? What would developers want or need to know to determine whether they could benefit from using the contents of your package? At the very least, we would need to have a list of the functions and procedures and what they do. For example, for each procedure, what values are computed and returned, and what parameters must be passed to perform these computations? This information forms the basis of the *package declaration*. It forms the interface or specification of the services that your package provides. When we write C or VHDL programs, we must declare the variables or signals that we are using—their type and possibly their initial values. Similarly, when we write packages, we must declare their contents. It is just that their contents are now more complex objects, such as functions, procedures, and data types. The package declaration is the means by which users declare what is available for use by VHDL programs. In the same sense that a hardware design unit possesses an external interface to communicate with other components, the package declaration defines the interface to other VHDL design units.

The easiest way to understand packages is by example, so let us examine a package that provides a new data type and a set of functions that operate on that data type. Throughout this text, the examples have declared and used the package `std_logic_1164.vhd`. Now let us look inside this package to see how the type is declared and how functions and declarations are used. Figure 13-7 shows a portion of the package declaration of an implementation of the

```
package std_logic_1164 is
-----------------------------------------------
    -- logic state system (unresolved)
-----------------------------------------------
type std_ulogic is ('U', -- Uninitialized
                     'X', -- Forcing Unknown
                     '0', -- Forcing 0
                     '1', -- Forcing 1
                     'Z', -- High Impedance
                     'W', -- Weak Unknown
                     'L', -- Weak 0
                     'H', -- Weak 1
                     '-' -- Don't care
                    );
type std_ulogic_vector is array (natural range <>) of
std_ulogic;

function resolved (s : std_ulogic_vector) return
std_ulogic;
subtype std_logic is resolved std_ulogic;

type std_logic_vector is array (natural range <>) of
std_logic;

function "and" (l, r : std_logic_vector) return
std_logic_vector;
function "and" (l, r : std_ulogic_vector) return
std_ulogic_vector;
  --
--..<rest of the package definition>
--
end std_logic_1164;
```

FIGURE 13-7 Examples from the package declaration of an implementation of the IEEE 1164 standard.

IEEE 1164 package distributed with the vast majority of the VHDL environments. The listing of the package declaration is provided in the VHDL reference manual provided in electronic form with the software. We know that the basic VHDL type **bit** can take on only values 0 and 1 and therefore is inadequate to represent most real systems. By using the concept of enumeration types (see "Enumeration Types," on page 232) a new type, std_ulogic, is defined as shown in Figure 13-7. Now a signal can be declared to be of this type:

signal *example_signal* : std_ulogic:='U';

The signal *example_signal* can now be assigned any one of the nine values defined previously rather than the two values 0 and 1. The package also declares a resolved type, std_logic, which is a subtype of std_ulogic. This declaration simply states that in the course of the simulation, when a signal of type std_logic is assigned a value, the resolution function resolved will be invoked to determine the correct value of a signal from the multiple drivers associated with the signal. However, we do have a problem in that all of the predefined logical functions, such as AND, OR, and XOR, operate on signals of type **bit**, which is predefined by the language. These logic functions must be redefined for signals std_logic type. Some of these functions are shown in Figure 13-7. The declarations of all of the functions provided in this package can be found in the VHDL reference manual provided in electronic form with the software. If we are constructing a package that uses types, procedures, or functions from another package, then access to this package must be provided via **library** and **use** clauses.

Now that we have defined what is in the package, we must provide the VHDL code that implements these functions and procedures. This implementation is contained in the *package body*. The package body is essentially a listing of the implementations. The body is structured as follows:

```
package body my_package is
--
-- type definitions, functions, and procedures
--
end my_package;
```

Once we have these packages, how do we use them? They are typically compiled and placed in *libraries* and referenced within VHDL design units via the **use** clause. All of the examples in this text have utilized the package std_logic_1164.vhd, which is in the library named IEEE. The essential properties of libraries are discussed next.

Essentials of Libraries

Each design unit—such as an entity, architecture, or package body—is analyzed (compiled) and placed in a *design library*. Libraries are generally implemented as directories and are referenced by a logical name. In the implementation of the VHDL simulator, this logical name maps to a physical path to the corresponding directory, and this mapping is maintained by the host implementation. However, just like variables and signals, before we can use a design library we must declare the library we are using by specifying the library's logical name. This is done using the **library** clause, which has the following syntax:

> **library** *logical-library-name-1,logical-library-name-2,...;*

In VHDL, the libraries STD and WORK are implicitly declared. Therefore, user programs do not need to declare these libraries. The former contains standard packages provided with VHDL distributions. The latter refers to the working directory, which can be set within the simulation environment you are using. Refer to your simulator documentation on how this can be done. However, if a program were to access functions in a design unit that was stored in a library with the logical name IEEE, then this library must be declared at the start of the program. Most, if not all, vendors provide an implementation of the library IEEE with packages such as std_logic_1164.vhd, as well as other mathematics and miscellaneous packages.

Once a library has been declared, all of the functions, procedures, and type declarations of a package in this library can be made accessible to a VHDL model through the **use** clause. For example, the following statements appear in all of the examples in this text:

> **library** IEEE;
> **use** IEEE.std_logic_1164.all;

The second statement makes *all* of the type definitions, functions, and procedures defined in the package std_logic_1164.vhd visible to the VHDL model. It is as if all of the declarations had been physically placed within the declarative part of a process that uses them. A second form of the **use** clause can be implemented when only a specific item, such as a function called `my_func`, in the package is to be made visible:

> **use** `IEEE.std_logic_1164.my_func;`

The **library** and **use** clauses establish the set of design units that is visible to the VHDL analyzer as it is trying to analyze and compile a specific VHDL design unit. When we first start writing VHDL programs, we tend to think of single entity–architecture pairs when constructing models. We probably organize our files in the same fashion, with one entity description and the associated architecture description in the same file. When this file is analyzed, the **library** and **use** clauses determine which libraries and packages within those libraries are candidates for finding functions, procedures, and user-defined types that are referenced within the model being compiled. However, these clauses apply only to the immediate design unit. *Visibility must be established for each design unit separately!* Every design unit must be preceded by **library** and **use** clauses as necessary. If we start having multiple design units within the same physical file, then each design unit must be preceded by the **library** and **use** clauses necessary to establish the visibility to the required packages.

Simulation Exercise 13.1: Packages and Libraries

This exercise concerns creating and using a simple package.

Step 1. Using a text editor, create a package with the following characteristics.

Several procedures for simulating a D flip-flop. You can start with the basic procedure given in "Positive-Edge-Triggered D Flip-Flop," on page 149, and modify it to produce procedures for the following:

– arguments of type **bit** and `std_logic`;

– arguments of type **bit_vector** and `std_logic_vector` (these are registers);

– use of reset and clear functions for different types of arguments.

Step 2. Analyze and test each of the procedures separately before committing them to placement within the package.

Step 3. Define a new type designed to represent a 32-bit register. This is simply a 32-bit object of the type `std_logic_vector`:

> **type** `register32` **is** `std_logic_vector` (31 **downto** 0);

Step 4. Propose and implement one or two other types of objects that you may expect to find in a model of a CPU or memory system.

Step 5. Create a library named MYLIB. This operation is usually simulator specific.

Step 6. Compile the package into the library MYLIB. This is typically done by setting the library WORK to be MYLIB. Your simulator documentation should provide guidelines on compiling design units into a library.

Step 7. Write a VHDL model of a bit-serial adder by using signals of type **bit** and adopting the structure shown in Figure 13-5. The model must declare the library MYLIB to provide access to your package via the **use** clause.

Step 8. Test the model of the bit-serial adder to ensure that it is functioning correctly.

Step 9. Modify the model to use signals of type std_logic. Nothing else should have to change, including the structure of the procedure call. By virtue of the argument type in the procedure call, the correct procedure in the package that you have written will be used.

Step 10. Modify the **use** clause to limit the visibility to one procedure in the package. Repeat your simulation experiments. You might have multiple instances of the **use** clause in order to provide visibility to each of the procedures you wish to utilize.

Step 11. Repeat the experiment to use other models of the D flip-flop that include signals such as reset and clear.

End Simulation Exercise 13.1

Chapter Summary

Designs can become large and complex. We need constructs that can help designers manage this complexity and enhance sharing of common design units. This chapter has addressed the essential issues governing the construction and use of subprograms: functions and procedures. Commonly used subprograms can be organized into packages and placed in design libraries for subsequent reuse and sharing across distinct VHDL models. The concepts introduced in this chapter include the following:

- Functions
  - ◆ type-conversion functions
  - ◆ resolution functions

- Procedures
  - ◆ concurrent procedure calls
  - ◆ sequential procedure calls
- Subprogram overloading
  - ◆ subprogram name
  - ◆ operator overloading
- Visibility rules
- Packages
  - ◆ package declaration
  - ◆ package body
- Libraries
  - ◆ relationships between design units and libraries

We are now armed with constructs for hiding complexity and sharing and reusing VHDL code modules.

Exercises

1. Create a package with functions and procedures for performing various shift operations and increment and decrement operations on **bit_vector** elements and `std_logic_vector` elements. Place the package declaration and package body in distinct files, and analyze them separately. Remember to declare and use the library `IEEE` and the package `std_logic_1164.vhd`.

2. Consider a VHDL type that can take on the values $(0, 1, X, U)$. The values X and U correspond to the values "unknown" and "uninitialized," respectively. Define a resolved type that takes on these values, and write and test a resolution function for this resolved type.

3. Write and test a set of procedures for performing arithmetic left- and right-shifts on vectors of type `std_logic_vector`.

4. Write and test a resolution function that operates on elements of type `std_logic_vector` and returns the largest value.

5. Write and test functions that can perform type conversion between multibit quantities of type `std_logic_vector` and integers.

6. Using a concurrent procedure looks very much like using a component in a hierarchically structured design. What is the difference between using a concurrent procedure and constructing a structural design?

7. Create a design library `My_Lib`, and place a package in this library. You might create a package of your own or simply "borrow" any one of a number of existing packages that come with VHDL environments. Analyze this package into this library. The creation of this library with the logical name `My_Lib` will involve simulator-specific operations. Ensure that you have correctly implemented this library by using elements of this package in a VHDL model analyzed into your working library, `WORK`.

14

Identifiers, Data Types, and Operators

The VHDL language provides a rich array of data types and operators, along with rules that govern their use. The goal of this chapter is to provide ready access to the syntax and semantics of the most commonly used data types and operators. This chapter is intended to serve more as a guide when writing your first VHDL programs than as a comprehensive language reference source. The more advanced language features are not referenced here, but can be found in a variety of excellent texts on the VHDL language. Familiarity with common programming-language concepts and idioms is assumed.

Identifiers

Identifiers are used as variable, signal, or constant names, as well as names of design units such as entities, architectures, and packages. A basic identifier is a sequence of characters that may be upper- or lowercase, the digits 0–9, or the underscore (_) character. The VHDL language is not case sensitive. The first character must be a letter, and the last character must not be "_". Therefore `Select`, `ALU_in`, and `Mem_data` are valid identifiers, while `12Select`, `_start`, and `out_` are not valid identifiers. Such identifiers are known as *basic identifiers*.

Data Objects

In VHDL, there are four types of objects: signals, variables, constants, and files.

NOTE: The file object type is not implemented in LogicWorks 5.

The range of values that can be assigned to a signal, variable, or constant object is determined by its type.

Signals

A signal is an object that holds the current and possibly future values of the object. In keeping with our view of VHDL as a language used to describe hardware, signals are typically thought of as representing wires. They occur as inputs and outputs in port descriptions, as signals in structural descriptions, and as signals in architectures. The signal declarations take the following form:

> **signal** *signal_name*: *signal_type*:= *initial_value*;

Examples include

> **signal** status : std_logic := '0';

and

> **signal** data : std_logic_vector (31 **downto** 0);

Recall that signals differ from variables in that signals are scheduled to receive values at some point in time by the simulator, while variables are assigned during execution of the assignment statement. At any given time, multiple values may be scheduled at distinct points in the future for a signal. In contrast, a variable can be assigned only one value at any point in time. As a result, the implementation of signal objects must maintain a history of values and therefore requires more storage and exact higher execution time overhead than variables.

Variables

Variables can be assigned a single value of a specific type. For example, an integer variable can be assigned a value in a range that is implementation dependent. A variable of type real can be assigned real numbers. Variables are essentially equivalent to their conventional-programming-language counterparts and are used for computations within procedures, functions, and processes. The declaration has the following form:

> **variable** *variable_name*: *variable_type* := *initial_value*;

Examples include the following:

> **variable** address: **bit_vector**(15 **downto** 0) := x"0000";
> **variable** Found, Done: **boolean** := FALSE;
> **variable** index: **integer range** 0 **to** 10:=0;

The last declaration states that the variable index is an integer that is restricted to values between 0 and 10 and is initialized to the value 0.

Constants

Constants must be declared and initialized at the start of the simulation and cannot be changed during the course of the simulation. Constants can be of any valid VHDL type. The declaration has the following form:

> **constant** *constant_name*: *constant_type* := *initial_value*;

Examples include the following:

> **constant** Gate_Delay: **time**:= 2 ns;
> **constant** Base_Address: **integer**:= 100;

The first declaration states that the constant is of type **time**. This is a type unique to hardware description languages. Just as an integer variable can be assigned only integer values, the values assigned to the constant Gate_Delay must be of type **time**, such as 5 ns, 10 ms, or 3 s. In the above example, Gate_delay is initialized to 10 ns.

Data Types

The type of a signal, variable, or constant object specifies the range of values it may take and the set of operations that can be performed on it. The VHDL language supports a standard set of type definitions as well as enables the definition of new types by the user.

The Standard Data Types

The standard type definitions are provided in the package STANDARD (see the VHDL Reference Manual provided in electronic form with the software) and include the types listed in Table 14-1. Note the definitions of **bit** and **bit_vector** types. From Chapter 9, we know that a simple 0/1 value system is not rich enough to describe the behavior of single-bit signals. This is why the community has moved towards standardization of a value system that multiple vendors can use. Such a standard is the IEEE 1164 value system, which is defined using enumeration types.

Enumeration Types

Although the standard types are useful for constructing a wide variety of models, they fall short in many situations. We know that single-bit signals may be in states that cannot be represented by 0/1 values. For example, signal values may be unknown, or signals may be left floating. The language does support the definition of new language types by the programmer and the ability to provide functions for operating on data that are of this type. For example, consider the following definition of a single bit:

```
type std_ulogic is ('U' -- uninitialized
    'X' -- forcing unknown
    '0' -- forcing 0
    '1' -- forcing 1
    'Z' -- high impedance
    'W' -- weak unknown
    'L' -- weak 0
    'H' -- weak 1
    '-' -- don't care
    );
```

Now assume that we declare a signal to be of this type:

TABLE 14-1 Standard data types provided within VHDL

Type	Range of Values	Example Declaration
integer	Implementation defined; LogicWorks uses 32-bit integers for a value range of −2147483647 to +2147483647.	**signal** index: **integer**:= 0;
real	Implementation defined; Not implemented in LogicWorks.	**variable** val: **real**:= 1.0;
boolean	True, False.	**variable** test: **boolean**:=TRUE;
character	Defined in package STANDARD.	**variable** term: **character**:= '@';
bit	0; 1.	**signal** In1: **bit**:= '0';
bit_vector	Array with each element of type bit.	**variable** PC: **bit_vector**(31 **downto** 0)
time	Implementation defined; LogicWorks uses 64-bit integers measured in femtoseconds, for a range of approximately 0 fs to 8,000 sec.	**variable** delay: **time**:= 25 **ns**;
string	Array with each element of type character.	**variable** name : **string**(1 **to** 10) := "model name";
natural	0 to the maximum integer value in the implementation.	**variable** index: **natural**:= 0;
positive	1 to the maximum integer value in the implementation.	**variable** index: **positive**:= 1;

signal carry:std_ulogic:='U';

The signal carry can now be assigned any one of the values previously defined. Note that operations such as AND, OR, +, and -- must be redefined for this data type. The type definitions and the associated operator and logical function definitions can be provided in a package that is referenced by your model. The above type definition is a standard defined by the IEEE, and the associated package is referred to as the IEEE Standard Logic 1164 package. (See the VHDL Reference Manual provided in electronic form with the software.) This package is popular for two reasons. First, it provides a type definition for signals that is more realistic for real circuits. Second, use of the same value system makes it easier for designers to share models, increasing interoperability and, consequently, reducing model cost.

The above type definition is referred to as an *enumeration type*. The definition explicitly enumerates all possible values that a variable or signal of this type can assume. Another example of where enumeration types come in handy is as follows:

type instr_opcode **is** (opADD, opSUB, opOR, opNOR, opBEQ);

An instruction-set simulation of a processor may have a large **case** statement with the following test:

case opcode **is**
when beq =>

Each branch of the **case** statement may call a procedure to simulate the execution of that particular instruction. Such type declarations can be made and placed in a package or in the declarative region of the **process**. For an example of the definition, declaration, and use of a type definition for memory in a simulation model of a simple processor, see the example code in "Modeling a Memory Module," on page 136.

Array Types

Arrays of bit-valued signals are common in digital systems. An array is a group of elements that are all of the same type. For example, a word is an array of bits, and memory is an array of words. A common practice is to define groups of interesting digital objects as a new type, such as in the following examples:

type byte **is array** (7 **downto** 0) **of bit**;
type word **is array** (31 **downto** 0) **of bit**;
type memory **is array** (0 **to** 4095) **of** word;

Now that we have created these new types, we can declare variables, signals, and constants to be of these types:

```
signal program_counter:word;= x"00000000";
variable data_memory:memory;
```

The use of type definitions in this manner enables us to define elements that we use when designing digital systems. For example, the preceding declarations demonstrate how we could define new types for words, registers, and memories. These new types make writing VHDL models more intuitive as well as easier to comprehend.

Physical Types

Physical types are motivated by the need to represent physical quantities such a time, voltage, or current. The values of a physical type are defined to be a measure, such as seconds, volts, or amperes. The VHDL language provides one predefined physical type: **time**. The definition of the type **time** can be found in the package STANDARD. The definition from this package is reproduced here:

```
type time is range <implementation dependent>
units
fs;          -- femtoseconds
ps = 1000 fs; -- picoseconds
ns = 1000 ps; -- nanoseconds
us = 1000 ns; -- microseconds
ms = 1000 us; -- milliseconds
s = 1000 ms; -- seconds
min = 60 s; -- minutes
hr = 60 min; -- hours
end units;
```

The first unit is referred to as the base unit and is the smallest unit of time. All of the other units can be defined in terms of any of the units defined earlier. For example, they all could have been defined in terms of femtoseconds.

NOTE: LogicWorks does not support user declaration of physical types.

Operators

Operators are used in expressions involving signal, variable, or constant object types. The following are the sets of operators as defined in the VHDL language:

logical operators	**and**	**or**	**nand**	**nor**	**xor**	**xnor**
relational operators	**=**	**/=**	**<**	**<=**	**>**	**>=**
shift operators	**sll**	**srl**	**sla**	**sra**	**rol**	**ror**
addition operators	**+**	**–**	**&**			
unary operators	**+**	**–**				
multiplying operators	*****	**/**	**mod**	**rem**		
miscellaneous operators	******	**abs**	**not**			

The miscellaneous operators include **abs** for the computation of the absolute value and ** for exponentiation. The latter can be applied to any integer or real signal, variable, or constant.

The classes of operators shown are listed in increasing order of precedence from top to bottom. Operators with higher precedence are applied to their operands first. All of the operators within the same class are of the same precedence and are applied to operands in textual order—left to right. The use of parentheses can be used to define explicitly the order of precedence. In general, the operands of these operators must be of the same type, whereas the type of the permissible operands may be limited. Table 14-2–14-7 provide information from the VHDL reference manual and define the permissible operand types:

TABLE 14-2 Operator–operand relationships

Operator	Operand Type	Result Type
=	Any type	Boolean
/=	Any type	Boolean
<, >, <=, >=	Scalar or discrete array types	Boolean

The shift operators are defined in Table 14-3. These operators are particularly useful in describing operations in models of computer architecture components. Some examples of the application of these shift operators are provided in Table 14-4.

NOTE: Although the VHDL language definition defines these operators only for **bit** and **boolean** types, the IEEE 1164 standard also defines them for arrays of **std_logic**.

TABLE 14-3 Shift operators

Operator	Operation	Left operand type	Right operand type	Result type
sll	Logical left shift	Any one dimensional array type whose element type is **bit** or **Boolean**	integer	left operand type
srl	Logical right shift	,,	,,	,,
sla	Arithmetic left shift	,,	,,	,,
sra	Arithmetic right shift	,,	,,	,,
rol	Rotate left logical	,,	,,	,,
ror	Rotate right logical	,,	,,	,,

TABLE 14-4 Examples of the application of the shift operators

Example expression	Result operand value
value <= "10010011" sll 2	"01001100"
value <= "10010011" sra 2	"11100100"
value <= "10010011" ror-3 (i.e., rotate left)	"10011100"
value <= "10010011" srl-2	"01001100"

TABLE 14-5 Addition and subtraction operators

Operator	Operation	Left Operand Type	Right Operand Type	Result Type
+ or −	Addition, subtraction	Numeric type	Same type	Same type
&	Concatenation	Array or element type	Array or element type	Same array type

The addition, subtraction, and concatenation operators are described in Table 14-5. The first two are self explanatory.

The concatenation operator composes operands. For example, we might have

result(31 **downto** 0) <= '0000' **&** jump (27 **downto** 0);

Here, the upper 4 bits of result will be cleared, and the remaining 28 bits will be set to the value of the 28 least significant bits of jump.

The unary operators are described in Table 14-6.

TABLE 14-6 Unary operators

Operator	Operation	Operand Type	Result Type
+/−	Identity, negation	Numeric type	Same type

Finally, some remaining numerical operators are illustrated in Table 14-7.

TABLE 14-7 Numerical operators

Operator	Operation	Left Operand Type	Right Operand Type	Result Type
*, /	Multiplication, division	Integer or floating point type	Same type	Same type
mod, rem	Modulus, remainder	Integer type	Same type	Same type

Chapter Summary

This chapter has provided a brief overview of the common objects, types, and operators in the VHDL language. I have taken the approach of focusing on the unique aspects of the VHDL language throughout most of the text, while assuming that language features such as types, identifiers, and objects, are familiar concepts to the reader and a handy reference is all that suffices as a prelude to writing useful models. This chapter is intended to fill that role and will be only as useful as the previous chapters have been successful in providing an intuitive way of thinking about, constructing, and using VHDL models. Familiarity at this level can lead to the next level in using the more powerful (and complex) features of the language.

Index